D1433212

SHIPWRECKS OF
THE ISLES OF SCILLY

SHIPWRECKS OF THE ISLES OF SCILLY

by

RICHARD LARN

Thomas & Lochar
PO Box 4, Nairn IV12 4HU

Acknowledgements

The Isles of Scilly have never had a daily news-paper as such, the nearest being a newsletter issued during the early part of W.W.2, and until the first telegraph cable was laid from the mainland in 1869, communications were both sporadic and intermittent, reliant entirely on mail carried by the various packet vessels, or word of mouth between travellers and fish-ermen reaching Penzance. The research neces-sary for this book was therefore conducted predominantly on the mainland, using West Country newspapers, or else the London Guildhall Library – the home of the Lloyds Collection, the Colinade Newspaper library, the Historic Manuscript Commission and Public Record Offices, at Kew and Chancery Lane; the British Library, State Paper and Round Rooms, and India Office Library. To the Superintendents and staff of all these estab-lishments, I offer my sincere appreciation and thanks for assistance. I also wish to particularly thank Barbara Jones, Senior Information Officer, Lloyds Register, her predecessor Jean Hood, and their staff for all their help and understanding.

I also extend thanks to C.J. Davies of Truro, a good friend, for the loan of his records; R Penhallurick, Curator, and H.L. Douch, past Curator of the Royal Institute of Cornwall; Miss R. Beckett, Falmouth Reference Library; Clive Carter of Penzance; John Behenna of Slapton, Devon; the late F.S. Dunn and Eric Collins. On Scilly, Steve Ottery, Curator of the islands' Museum, Roy Graham, David McBride and the late John Osborne. To Frank Gibson, for permission to use photographs from his family collection, also to the *Western Morning News*, Plymouth for photographs, and HMSO Hydrographic Department MOD (Navy), Taunton, particularly Lt Cdr John Pugh RN Ret'd, Wrecks Officer.

To Pat and Padriac Keady, of Palmers Green, who often sacrifice their own bed, when we stay with them on research visits, and always make us welcome, as have Tony & Francis Taylor and John & Jane Selby.

Finally, to Bridget, my wife and constant companion, who actually likes shipwreck research, and plays a major role in our writing activities.

Richard Larn, Charlestown, Cornwall 1992

Previous page: A bewildered steer wandering around the rocks of Crebawethan, one of the 250 animals rescued from the wreck of the SS. *Castleford* on 8 June 1887, after she stranded in dense fog.

British Library Cataloguing in Publication Data

Larn Richard.
Shipwrecks of The Isles of Scilly –
2 Rev. ed
  I. Title II. Carter, Clive
  363.1230942379

ISBN 0 946537 84 4

© RICHARD LARN 1993

All rights reserved. No part of this publication may be reproduced, stored in a retrieval system, or trans-mitted, in any form or by any means, electronic, mechanical, photocopying, recording or otherwise, without the prior permission of the publisher.

Typeset by XL Publishing Services, Nairn
Printed in Great Britain
by Redwood Books, Trowbridge
for Thomas & Lochar
PO Box 4, Nairn, Scotland IV12 4HU

Contents

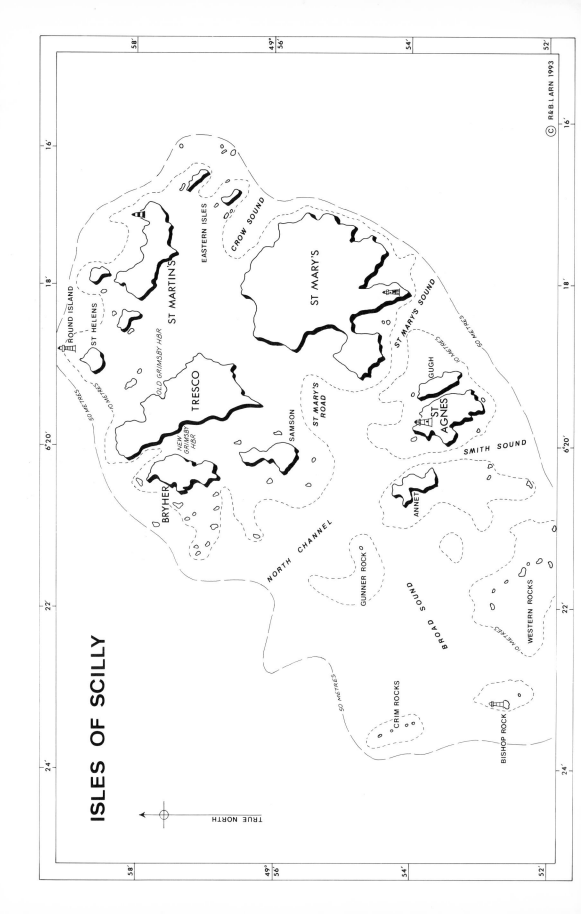

ISLES OF SCILLY

TRUE NORTH

© R&B LARN 1993

Introduction

The 1971 edition of this volume, *Cornish Shipwrecks – the Isles of Scilly*, the second in a Cornish trilogy, was a double first. Primarily it was the first book to record in detail the shipwrecks of Scilly; it was also the very first book I wrote alone. In hindsight, I was still very inexperienced, allowing a number of inexcusable mistakes to be printed. I should also have carried out more research, and employed a professional proof-reader to vet the manuscript.

Now, twenty-one years later, certainly older and hopefully wiser, I have the opportunity to make up for the shortcomings of that first edition. If anything, I consider myself privileged to be writing this second edition, many authors do not get such an opportunity, and I would like to acknowledge publicly my gratitude to three individuals who directly or indirectly made this and other books possible, and literally changed my life. The first of these was the late Joan du Platt Taylor, a professional archaeologist, who founded nautical archaeology in this country, and introduced me to the Devon publishers, David & Charles, with the reassuring words, 'anyone can write a book'!

The second person was the late Theodore Stanhope Sprigg, director and editor of that company, who gave me a contact for *Cornish Shipwrecks – the South Coast*, before I had even produced a synopsis or written one single word. His confidence was not misplaced, since we produced five shipwreck books before he died. Lastly, this and other publications would never have happened without the approval and backing of David St John Thomas, co-founder and later chairman of David & Charles, who in 1991 set off for Nairn, Scotland, and started an entirely new publishing company. To him in particular, my grateful thanks.

Public interest and awareness of shipwreck has greatly increased over the past twenty years, so much so that recording and writing about shipwrecks, and displaying shipwreck artefacts has become our full-time occupation. A revised look at the 700 or so wrecks around the Isles of Scilly is therefore timely.

Richard & Bridget Larn
Charlestown, Cornwall. 1992

1

Living from the sea

It is a fact that of all the many islands and island groups around Great Britain, none of equal size or population are as exposed or remote as the Isles of Scilly. Amongst the Western Isles of Scotland, Orkney or Shetland, there are many remote communities, but all much closer to large, well-populated towns or mainland Scotland than St Mary's is to Penzance or Land's End. The west coast of Ireland also has its island communities, but they too enjoy a closer proximity to the mainland, albeit that coastline like Scotland's, can be very desolate. Lundy Island in the Bristol Channel probably equates best geographically to the Scillies, but its population is not even the equal of the tiny island of St Agnes or Bryher, and is roughly only 22 miles from a mainland port compared to 42 miles for St Mary's. Lundy is also equally exposed to the weather, is in a busy shipping lane, was once a haven for pirates, has seen many shipwrecks, and has a history of a long succession of absentee landlords, but there the similarity ends.

The heritage of all islanders is the sea, the element which will dictate their fortunes, their way of life, their very existence. For many people island life might appear idyllic, but even the smallest stretch of sea separating islands can impose enormous problems and a particular way of life, and a remoteness that for some may become insufferable. Described variously as the 'Fortunate Islands' or the 'Isles of Flowers', for the Isles of Scilly these are modern sentimentalities, uttered safe in the knowledge that there is now a reliable supply of mains electricity, that the telephone links the islands with the outside world, that there is now – for the first time in its long history – an adequate fresh water supply. Also, that aircraft and the Scillonian III will bring the essential visitors which now form the island's main economy, or transfer a patient to a mainland

hospital within 30 minutes, and that in the event of cataclysmic disaster, either HM Government or EEC funds would instantly be available. But it has not always been so; for the greater part of its history a more suitable description might well be the 'unfortunate islands', and the occupants of Scilly must often have cursed the sea, for whilst it provided the majority with a living – and everyone must have derived some benefit from it, it isolated them from the prosperity and progress of the mainland. On several occasions real starvation was only narrowly averted by the generosity of those living in west Cornwall. In one instance the much treasured coat of arms from the wreck of HM Man o'war *Association* (1707) was presented to Penzance in appreciation of assistance, which now hangs in their Guildhall. Successive monarchs since the time of Edgar and their respective governments were inclined to forget the Scillies even existed. Only when it was time to levy more taxes, or in time of war when there was a chance they might be captured by a foreign power, were they acknowledged and garrisoned, and then only until such time as the crisis was resolved. The industrial revolution passed them by completely, the islands benefiting only from a short-lived period of shipbuilding in the mid to late 1800s, and only in the last 60 years have the islands enjoyed good communications with the mainland and other commonplace amenities.

Following his visit to the islands in 1724, Daniel Defoe, the novelist and pamphleteer, in his 'Tour Through Gt Britain' wrote: 'These islands be so in the middle between the two vast openings that it cannot, or perhaps never will be avoided.' He referred, of course, to the Scillies' position at the apex of two major shipping routes, the English and Bristol Channels, or Severn Sea, as it was then known – and shipwrecks. The former gave access to the south coast ports, the capital and the North sea, the latter to the vast armada of ships that carried coal from the South Wales ports, copper and tin from north Cornwall, and more exotic cargoes to and from Bristol. Defoe in fact could equally well have written of '... three vast openings', since Scilly is equally the signpost for north bound sea traffic coming up from Biscay seeking St George's Channel and the Irish Sea, overall a vast sea traffic which for well over 300 year gave employment to Scilly pilots.

Low lying in the extreme, the highest part of St Mary's being only 57m above sea level, the Scillies comprise some 145 islands and major rocks of which only five are now inhabited. Spread out so as to offer a ten mile wide barrier lying north-east/south-west, they once presented quite a fearsome barrier to ships, which have in the past claimed several wrecks in a single day and continue to claim the occasional vessel, although there has not been a shipwreck on Scilly of any significance since the *Enfant de Bretagne* in 1977, and *Le Resolu* on the Seven Stones in 1980. The fact that the islands have such a low silhouette, and that the majority of the rocks and outlying reefs are covered at high-water, has been the direct cause of the majority of ship losses. When shrouded in fog or rain, the entire island group can merge into a background of heaving grey sea, and many a lookout on board sailing ships and steamers alike, lulled into a stupor after several hours of seeing nothing but their own indistinct bow in front of them, saw breakers ahead only when it was too late. 'The three Ls' was the favourite expression of early sailing masters when instructing their juniors, meaning latitude, lead line and lookout, as they approached land. Latitude could be readily calculated, so that the master would know how far north or south his ship was on the globe, but determining longitude at sea, ie east/west position, defied man's ingenuity until 1765. Even then chronometers were not readily available for sea-going ships until the mid 1800s, and any form of navigation is only as good as the sea chart on which the ship's progress is marked. In the early eighteenth century, the Isles of Scilly, despite having been surveyed by the Dutch – then considered to be the best chart makers in the world – were shown between fifteen and twenty miles further north than they actually were, and everyone was ignorant of what today is known as the Rennell Current which sweeps these waters. As to the lead line, it was necessary to take the way off the ship by taking in sail before a reasonably accurate 'plumb' of the sea could be obtained, the minute sample of seabed material brought up stuck in the 'arming' tallow assisting in determining a location, but again if the chart was inaccurate it was all basically guesswork. The last resort therefore was the lookout, and around the Scillies, the dice was often loaded against the mariner. Today, with sophisticated electronic aids to navigation, it is difficult to imagine ships wandering the oceans with only a vague idea as to their position, but such was often the case. Two classic examples illustrate the point, the first concerning a homeward-bound fleet of English East Indiamen in 1703 who, 'thought they were in the English Channel making for Portsmouth but sighted and recognised Lundy before discovering their mistake.' The second concerns a French 64-gun, second-rate man o'war, the *Belliquex*, on passage from Quebec in 1758, which sailed right up the Bristol Channel to Lundy and into the surprised arms of a British fleet, her captain still under the fond delusion that Brest, his destination, lay just ahead.

In the eighteenth century, wrecks around Scilly were probably so frequent that they were taken for granted, and at the time no one could imagine things would ever change. Exactly how many ships have gone down hereabouts will never be known for certain, since perhaps 50 could have been lost at night amongst the Western Rocks over a 400 year period, leaving no trace by morning, any floating evidence having gone away on the tide. One writer debited the islands with 200 wrecks during the past 150 years, another with 75 between 1878 and 1927, whereas the true figures are 365 and 189 respectively for those periods. Early writers made frequent mention of the wrecks on Scilly: John Troutbeck in 1796 wrote that the

Scillonians 'are, by their situation, the sons and daughters of God's providence and accordingly are otherwise cloathed and supplied out of wrecks sent in by the sea, the spoil of their rich neighbours'. Sir Walter Besant in 1860 claimed that 'every rock in Scilly has a shipwreck' – but how many that was supposed to be is anyone's guess! This book contains an index of 666 known wrecks, the most comprehensive and near definitive record possible after exhaustive, experienced research into almost every source over many years. Unfortunately, the fate of ships listed merely as 'missing', whose track would have taken them close to Scilly after sailing from a UK or foreign port may never be solved, and hence this list must remain forever only near definitive. Readers may well question this number of shipwrecks, wondering how it compares with other areas, particularly mainland Cornwall for example. The number of wrecks on Scilly is relatively small, compared with over 1,400 and 1,900 losses on the north and south coasts of mainland Cornwall respectively, which has a coastline of some 300 miles in total.

Ships cast ashore 500 years ago were considered of such little importance in themselves, that their names were seldom if ever recorded, which is strange considering there were far fewer vessels sailing the sea, and their relative cost at the time. What was important was their contents, often very valuable, which led to 'Right of Wreck', an exceptionally lucrative and jealously guarded perquisite of rich landowners usually at the expense of the ship or cargo owner. 'Right of Wreck', which dates back to the Roman conquest since its origins are enshrined in Rhodian Law, refers to the legal beneficiary of shipwreck in a particular area, regardless of whether the item concerned was a whole or part ship, its stores or cargo, as well as whale, dolphins and porpoise washed up on the foreshore. The fact that this legal expression has survived through the ages to the present day, and probably appears more often in State and legal documents than any other, demonstrates the great financial benefit and value placed on this ancient and infamous privilege

which was strongly defended. It is interesting that as late as 1992, a Mr A.J.B. Mildmay-White, of Mothercombe House, Devon, brought a case before the Department of Transport, claiming manorial Right of Wreck for his estate which overlooks the River Erme estuary in Bigbury Bay. An historic wreck site had been found on the Mary reef in the estuary, and in the dispute regarding ownership the Crown conceded Mildmay-White's claim to artefacts recovered.

In Scilly, the Right of Wreck, taken as being vested in the English crown in the first place, passed to the church in 1114. Although Scilly is not mentioned in the Doomsday Book, Henry I granted the Abbot of Tavistock 'all the churches of Sully with their appurtenances.' At a later date, Reginald, the Earl of Cornwall confirmed the grant with the amendment 'All the wrecks, except whale and a whole ship.' Although not the first Christian monks on the islands – there is the legend that Olaf Tryggvesson, king of Norway as it was then, came to Scilly in 989 and was converted to Christianity by holy men already there – the priory on Tresco, then St Nicholas Isle, brought some semblance of law and order to the otherwise lawless islands. Piracy was one of their biggest problems, and it is recorded that on Ascension Day 1209, 'pirates were beheaded in St Nicholas Isle in Sully to the number of one hundred and twelve'. In 1302, Edward I, desirous of obtaining the coveted Right of Wreck for himself, challenged the Tavistock abbot, but a jury found that 'the abbot and all his predecessors had enjoyed wreck from time immemorial, except for whales, gold, scarlet cloth, masts and firs, which were reserved for the king.'

If dispute arose few if any complaints would reach London, and any that did were probably so outdated by the time they reached the royal court as to be difficult to act upon. The seat of government necessitated five days somewhat hazardous journey on horseback from Penzance, always provided the weather allowed a boat passage from Scilly. As late as 1744, passage between St Mary's and Penzance was seldom made more than once a month in summer, and less frequently in winter. To quote Lieut Heath, 1750, 'in small boats, amidst the running of several cross tides, the passengers are forced to venture at the extreme hazard of their lives when only the necessity or duty calls them'. Even by 1822, a crossing could still be an alarming experience, as one old lady from St Mary's, visiting relatives on the mainland, was to discover. After a sea passage lasting over twenty-four hours, the boat was forced by stress of weather into Mousehole, and the old lady had to walk the last three miles to her destination.

One case of plunder in Scilly which was brought directly to the attention of London occurred in 1305 concerning William Le Poer, the coroner for Scilly. Lieut Heath, in his *Natural & Historical Account of the Isles of Scilly*, 1750, quotes from a letter from Edward I:

We understand by the grevious Complaint of William Le Poer, our Coroner in the Islands of Scilly, belonging to our County of Cornwall, that whereas he lately, for the Preservation of the Peace at La Val, Trescaw, in the islands aforesaid, did repair to enquire of Manslaughter, Robberies, Incendiaries, and other Felonies: and Receivers of Goods feloniously stolen; and of Wreck of the Sea, as to the said office appertaineth. Ranulph De Blackminster; Michael Petit; Edmund Speccot; John Gabbere; Robert Abbat of Tavistock; Frier, John De Yalineton; Frier, John of Exeter; and Oliver of Scilly, Chaplain, the aforesaid Coroner, by force of Arms, imprisoned, ill used, and there did maliciously procure him to be kept, at the said Town of de La Val, until such time as the said Coroner paid a fine to the said Ranulph, Michael, Edmund, John, Abbat; John, John and Oliver, and the Malefactors aforesaid, of 100 shillings for his enlargement out of the prison aforesaid.

In 1337 the Right of Wreck in Scilly reverted to the crown, when Edward III endowed his son Edward, the Black Prince, with the Duchy of Cornwall, a relationship between the county, the islands and the monarchy which continues to this day. Whilst some may imagine that the Duchy embraces all Cornwall, in fact it has only ever owned seventeen per cent of the mainland area, but historically 100 percent of the Isles of Scilly, although all Hughtown and some other properties on St Mary's are now freehold. Five years after the initial grant, in 1342, the prince was complaining to his father that 'certayn persons have helped themselves to my priveleages, to £1,000 worth of goods'. A similar letter followed a year later, this time the sum being £3,000, and again in 1345 'goods to the value of 2,000 marks were missing, the rightful perquisite of the prince, stolen on the spot'. As mentioned earlier, the value of the wreck goods was the sole concern, with no mention of the ship's name or consideration for the owner of the cargo of 'goods'. So it continued, both on the mainland and amongst the islands, wreck after wreck, the locals describing their activities on the foreshore or amongst the Western Rocks as 'a-shoring', rather than 'wrecking'.

In 1536 Henry VIII created a vice-admiral for both Devon and Cornwall, a position held only by gentlemen or nobles. Seventeen years later the counties were separated into vice-admiralties, but the Scillies were omitted, leased instead to Frances Godolphin in 1571 for the annual sum of twenty pounds. Previously, successive 'lords' of Scilly, namely Blanchminster, Denver, Whittington, the Coleshill's and Arundell's, had all used the islands to their own ends, whereas the coming of the Godolphin's at last brought to an end what has best been described as 'the islands' awful period'.

Wrecking is an expression which has two definitions, related but infinitely different in execution. A modern dictionary defines a 'wrecker' as 'a person who purposely causes a wreck, or, one who plunders a wreck'. Whilst there is ample evidence of looting and plunder of shipwrecks by Scillonians and Cornishmen alike, there is not one documented case of a ship being lured by false lights whether 'tied to donkey's tails' or not. In fact the only known case in the country to come before a magistrate's court of displaying false lights was in 1773 at Anglesey. That is not to say that no Cornishman ever deliberately lured a ship ashore, but simply that there is no proof either way. For a long time it was generally accepted that no Cornish jury would ever convict a fellow countryman on a charge of wrecking, but the exception was proved in 1767. Mr Justice Yates, either at Bodmin or Launceston, sentenced a wrecker to death and 'improved the occasion by addressing not the prisoner but the court against so savage a crime'. Every effort was made to save the man's life, the MP for Launceston putting pressure on the Secretary for State, Lord Shelborne, by reminding him that feelings were high in the wrecker's favour and that an election was due soon! Nevertheless, the man was duly hanged, one of the few cases on record of the death penalty being administered for stealing from a wreck.

During his visit to Scilly in 1724 mentioned earlier, when Daniel Defoe remarked upon 'the two great openings', he also wrote:

'– the sands covered in people, they are charged with strange bloody and cruel dealings, even sometimes with one another, but especially with poor distressed seamen who seek for help for their lives and find the rocks themselves not more cruel and merciless than the people who range about them for their prey.'

Borlase, in 1756, saw islanders stripping the clothes off the back of a shipwrecked mariner, found half drowned on the foreshore, and the man was probably lucky to have been left alive. Legally, if a man or dog escaped alive from a ship it was not considered a wreck; a peculiar technicality going back to Rhodian Sea Law and the Rolls of Orlean that surely could be interpreted as an open invitation to commit murder? More than one hundred years after Defoe's visit to Scilly, in their report of 15 August 1836, the 'Select Committee Appointed to inquire into the Causes of Shipwreck'

reported to Parliament, 'whilst on other parts of the English coast persons assemble by hundreds for plunder on the occurrence of a wreck, on the Cornish coast they assemble in their thousands'. In Scilly of course, there was insufficient population to assemble in such numbers, but it was certainly true of Mount's Bay and the St Ives area in Cornwall, where tin miners would congregate literally in thousands from miles around at the scene of a wreck. When a family was living at near starvation level or the children were without boots or warm clothing in winter, if a man helped himself to foodstuffs otherwise going to waste in the shallows, or removed the shirt and boots from a corpse to help the living – in cases of abject poverty and dire need – who could blame them? As far as the 'wrecker' was concerned, the dead had no use for clothing, but regrettably, the law had no time for sentiment or personal circumstances.

Wrecks represented gain in many different forms, and no Scillonian could afford to miss an opportunity to make a few shillings, or improve their lot. The variety of goods carried in ships is infinite; food, timber, paint, flour, soap, clothes, iron, wire, leather, even pencils, it could all be put to some use, bartered or sold, and a whole house could be furnished from a wreck, down to carpets, stove, lamps, bedsteads, even a piano!

For merely being the first to bring news of a wreck to the receiver at the Custom House in Hughtown, brought a reward of five-shillings, and often relatively large sums would be awarded by the owner of a derelict or damaged ship towed in and saved, which would be shared amongst those responsible. One example in 1880 concerned the saving of the schooner *Strathisla* after she had been abandoned by her crew. For getting the vessel into St Mary's, the pilot-gig *Bernice*, and the pilot-cutters *Atlantic* and *Presto* were awarded £48, and for saving the crew, the gig *Agnes* received £15. On 24 October 1878, when the SS *Ely Rise* stranded in Crow Sound, some 30-40 pilots were employed to save the provisions and furniture on board, for which they claimed

The SS *Castleford*, from Montreal for London, stranded on Crebawethan, amongst the Western Rocks, whilst travelling at full-speed in fog on 8 June 1887. Amongst her general cargo were 460 head of cattle, the greater part of which drowned.

£100. Unfortunately, the event was marred by the theft of £200 worth of property and £80 worth of provisions, and the coastguards were put on watch. That night, officer McGillicuddy doing his rounds on St Martin's came across a dozen men, laden with stolen goods. They dropped everything and ran, except for James Nance, who lay down and tried to hide but was apprehended; a warrant was issued for his arrest but on hearing of it he jumped into his boat and sailed off to the mainland! When the SS *Castleford* was lost amongst the Western Rocks in 1887, £12.11s went to St Agnes for saving eighteen cattlemen and £500 to Bryher men for the rescue and care of sixty-six passengers and four stewardesses, plus £5 for every head of cattle saved and £1 for every corpse buried on the foreshore. Such sums were almost untold wealth for the Scillonians, and many families literally earned their living from the sea in this way.

Unfortunately, no written account of what it was like to be wrecked on Scilly has been passed down from a mariner, unlike Devon and Dorset where quite graphic accounts survive. The coast of mainland Cornwall abounds with sandy beaches, on which a vessel could be driven if in distress, with every chance the ship and crew would survive, but not so on Scilly. In even a moderate sea and swell, the Western Rocks, by far the most dangerous waters locally, are a quite fearful and dangerous place. In a howling south-westerly gale, with mountainous seas breaking over seemingly endless reefs and shoals, turning the surface into one mass of broken white water with rocks showing their black heads in all directions, a shipwrecked crew must have thought they had

sailed into hell. With their ship literally being torn to pieces beneath their feet by the constant heave and surge of gigantic waves. The rigging offered the only remaining sanctuary, until the chain plates gave way, the masts fell, and men already half frozen and near unconscious from exposure plunged into a gelid sea. Few people at that time could swim, and those that could would be hampered by heavy sodden clothing and leather seaboots, so that the majority would drown. Others would find floating wreckage to which they clung, fighting for air as wave after wave passed over them, doing their best to get away from the rocks that could break a limb and inflict severe lacerations. If they were lucky, a local boat might put out when the weather eased and rescue them, or they might be unlucky, and get swept far out to sea with the tide, to meet a lonely, pitiless death. Survivors would generally be well received ashore but not always, and if foreign, language difficulties often made communication impossible; they probably had no conception as to where they were, no money, and no idea of what to do next. A short uncomfortable sea crossing and they were thrust ashore in another strange country, where times were hard and few would help a shipwrecked mariner. How such unfortunates got back to their homes in Venice or Lisbon, St Petersburg or Ghent, defies imagination, since they were faced with travelling the width of the country, finding a ship to cross the channel, then making their way across Europe. They must frequently have been given up for dead, arriving back home months, perhaps even years later.

The history of Scilly has been one of constant change, from periods of stability, relative wealth and peace, to extreme hardship, always dictated by the sea. Usually, no sooner did a little prosperity appear than the source or demand would vanish, and the people were reduced once more to hard times. It is remarkable that the islands remained inhabited for certain periods, but the people of Scilly were a hardy breed who knew from bitter experience how to weather a storm in more than one sense. When the price of burned kelp fell, or the pilchards and herrings disappeared, there was always the sea. When steamships ousted sail and deprived the pilots of their living, and the islands lost the revenue brought by the hundreds of sailing ships which would otherwise have crowded the roads; when the shipbuilding ceased because iron was taking the place of wood; when the hopes of a coaling station, and then the Royal Navy making Broad Sound into a heavily defended fleet anchorage came to nothing, there was always the sea. Even today, the current prosperity of the islands can be directly attributed to the sea that isolates it from the mainland, its main attraction to holiday makers being its isolation and unspoilt character. Its flower and potato industry may be in decline, unable to compete with even crops grown in Cornwall due to high freight charges, but the farmers have adapted to the tourist trade, and life goes on. Seldom does the sea bring a shipwreck these days, although gales lash the islands with the same violence they did 250 years ago, and fog makes their outline just as indistinct. Little has changed in fact, except that man has learnt better to predict the elements, and master them at sea.

Opposite: A bronze cannon recovered from the wreck of Dutch East Indiaman *Hollandia,* which sank off George Peter's Ledge, Annet, 3 July 1743. The breech area bears the mark of the Amsterdam Chamber of the company (VOC).

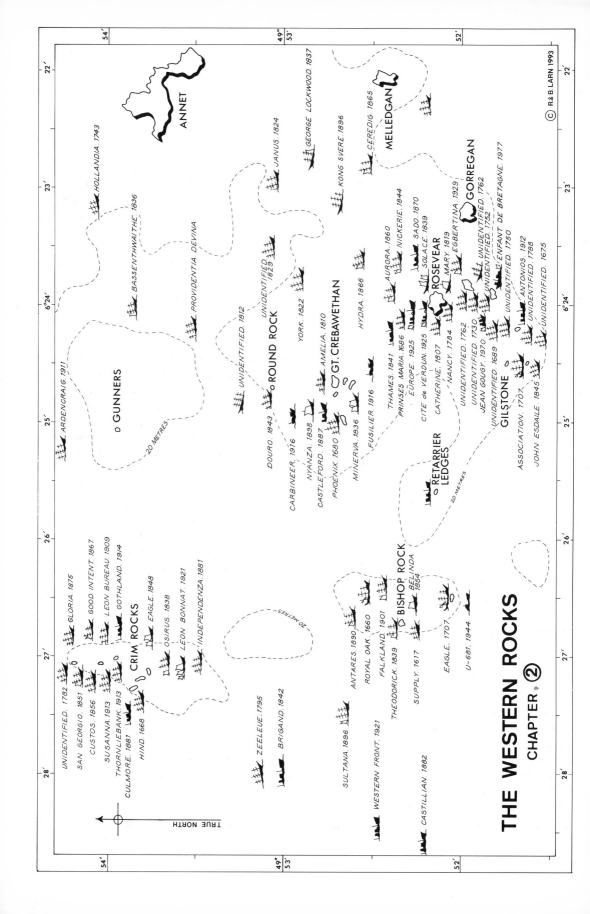

THE WESTERN ROCKS
CHAPTER, ②

© R & B LARN 1993

ANNET

HOLLANDIA. 1743

BASSENTHWAITHE. 1836

PROVIDENTIA DEVINA

GEORGE LOCKWOOD. 1837

KONG SVERE. 1896

JANUS. 1824

CEREDIG. 1865

MELLEDGAN

GORREGAN

ARDENCRAIG. 1911

○ GUNNERS

20 METRES

UNIDENTIFIED. 1812

UNIDENTIFIED 1829

○ ROUND ROCK

YORK. 1822

AMELIA. 1810

GT. CREBAWETHAN

HYDRA. 1866

AURORA. 1860

NICKERIE. 1844

SADO. 1870

SOLACE. 1839

ROSEVEAR

MARY. 1819

EGBERTINA. 1929

UNIDENTIFIED. 1752

UNIDENTIFIED. 1762

L'ENFANT DE BRETAGNE. 1977

DOURO. 1843

CARBINEER. 1916

NYANZA. 1898

CASTLEFORD. 1887

PHOENIX. 1680

MINERVA. 1836

FUSILIER. 1916

THAMES. 1841

PRINSES MARIA. 1686

EUROPE. 1925

CITE de VERDUN. 1925

CATHERINE. 1807

NANCY. 1784

UNIDENTIFIED. 1762

UNIDENTIFIED. 1730

JEAN GOUGY. 1970

UNIDENTIFIED. 1689

ANTONIOS. 1912

UNIDENTIFIED. 1788

UNIDENTIFIED. 1675

GILSTONE

UNIDENTIFIED. 1750

○ RETARRIER LEDGES

20 METRES

ASSOCIATION. 1707

JOHN ESDAILE. 1845

UNIDENTIFIED. 1782

SAN GEORGIO. 1851

CUSTOS. 1856

SUSANNA. 1913

THORNLIEBANK. 1913

CULMORE. 1881

HIND. 1668

GLORIA. 1875

GOOD INTENT. 1867

LEON BUREAU. 1909

GOTHLAND. 1914

EAGLE. 1848

OSIRUS. 1838

LEON BONNAT. 1921

INDEPENDENZA. 1881

CRIM ROCKS

20 METRES

ZEELEUE. 1795

BRIGAND. 1842

ANTARES. 1890

ROYAL OAK. 1660

FALKLAND. 1901

THEODORICK. 1839

SUPPLY. 1617

○ BISHOP ROCK

BELINDA. 1864

EAGLE. 1707

U-681. 1944

SULTANA. 1896

WESTERN FRONT. 1921

CASTILLIAN. 1882

TRUE NORTH

54'

22'

23'

6°24'

25'

26'

27'

28'

49° 53'

52'

54'

49° 53'

52'

2

The infamous Western Rocks

IT is doubtful if any collection of rocks in the whole of the British Isles has a worse reputation than that to the west of St Agnes. Known collectively as the Western Rocks, this immense area of hidden danger covers almost ten square miles, and has been the setting for the worst of the many wreck disasters at Scilly. Prior to 1680, when the islands were marked by neither light nor beacon, the toll of shipping between St Agnes and the Bishop and Clerks, as the outer rocks were then known, must have been nothing short of appalling. Even after the coal-fired beacon on St Agnes had been erected and lit, the Western Rocks continued to claim ships almost as if they had some magical attraction.

When it became obvious that a warning light further west was essential, a more powerful and reliable light than St Agnes, there were serious misgivings as to the choice of site. The fact that the Bishop Rock was chosen on which to erect the new lighthouse is testimony in itself to the respect men had for this mass of rock and reef. Of the many available sites on which to build, there could hardly be one more difficult or exposed on which to carry out such a feat of engineering. Only two miles to the east lie Rosevear and Rosevean, infinitely more sheltered and suitable one might think, but unfortunately neither mark the extreme westerly limit of the Scillies. Between them and the open Atlantic lie the Gilstone Reef, Retarrier Ledges, Crebinicks, the Crims and finally Bishop Rock itself, all of which have taken a fearful toll of life and property over the centuries. Exactly how the Bishop acquired its name is uncertain; one explanation states they derived their name from an incident which happened 200 years ago, when a fleet of merchantmen coming from Spain were shipwrecked on them (the Bishop and Clerks), and only Miles Bishop and John and Henry Clerk were preserved on a fragment of a mast.[1]

The first lighthouse on the Bishop was designed by James Walker and built by Nicholas and James Douglass between 1848 and 1850, but it proved a failure. Unlike the present-day lighthouse, with its slender stone structure, the first light was atop an open construction made of cast iron. A central pillar, 3ft 6in in diameter, carried an entrance door and ladder by which access was gained to the keepers' quarters and light platform, 120 ft above sea level, the whole being supported by wrought-iron stays secured to bed rock. The onset of winter in 1849 brought work on the structure to an end, it being the intention to complete the light the following spring. But disaster struck during the night of 5 February 1850 when the entire framework was swept away by a severe gale. It was not the method of fastening the column to the rock which had been at fault, but the inadequate tensile strength of the materials used. Ten days elapsed before anyone could approach the Bishop Rock to inspect the damage, which showed that the stays and central column had sheared between 3 and 5ft from their base.

Undaunted by failure, Trinity House remained firm in their confidence in the Douglass combination of father and son, and by early 1852 a new structure began to rise above the rock. This time the tower was constructed of granite, great blocks hewn from the quarries of Carnsew and Lamorna in Cornwall, ferried first to St Mary's to be dressed and then to the Bishop in the sailing tender *Billow*, and later in barges towed by the tug *Bishop*. Rosevear, an uninhabited island, was chosen as a base for the workmen and engineers, and a number of stone buildings were erected. This was, in fact, the second time Rosevear had been utilised as a base camp, since it was from here that the Herbert salvage expedition of 1709-10 worked the wreck of the

Association and other vessels in Sir Clowdisley Shovell's fleet of 1707. Work continued on the lighthouse throughout 1852, often under appalling conditions, and it was not until the solid base had reached a height of 45ft above sea level that the workmen could relax their vigilance a little. Whilst the first granite blocks were being keyed into the base rock, the labourers were often completely engulfed by the sea when huge waves broke over them. The stonemasons worked in permanently wet clothes, and on more than one occasion were washed clean off the rock into the boiling surf. By the end of 1852, forty-four blocks had been laid, and the vital lower stones securely dovetailed into the natural rock.

Upon completion, the tower reached a height of 131 ft above high-water mark and, when the light was first displayed on 1 September 1858, it was visible for fourteen miles. Four keepers were employed to maintain the light, three on duty at any one time, the fourth ashore in rotation, and their occupation was not one to be envied. The Bishop lighthouse is one of the most exposed lights in the country, and the damage inflicted on the structure during its first baptism by storm on 30 January 1860 showed the destructive force of the sea to its full. The massive metal ladder and door which gave access to the interior were swept away, windows 5in thick were smashed, glass prisms in the light broken and the tower flooded. The huge fog bell, weighing a little over a quarter of a ton, was washed away from the gallery and fell onto the rocks below. In falling it may well have smashed, but there is no record of it ever being found and it is assumed to still lie on the seabed at the base of the Bishop, amongst the wreckage of the many ships lost there.

In September 1870, the lighthouse was again battered by a severe gale — if anything,

Opposite: The famous Bishop Rock lighthouse, the last of the west country lighthouses to remain manned, which became fully automatic on 21 December 1992. The helicopter landing platform which assisted crew changes in bad weather will still be used by occasional maintenance crews.

worse than the one of ten years earlier — which sent seas completely over the lantern from eight o'clock in the morning until two in the afternoon; and on 20 April 1874 it was subjected to an even more trying test. When that gale was over, the keepers stated that waves had reached the level of the kitchen window 70ft above the sea and had broken clean over the lantern, bathing the interior of the light in a ghostly green glow. Had the storm continued with equal violence for another twenty-four hours the entire structure might well have been endangered, possibly destroyed. As it was, the exterior was considerably damaged and had to be repaired that year. Subsequently between 1882 and 1887, the lighthouse was enveloped in a new stone casing dovetailed both vertically and horizontally, and the overall height increased by 36ft. This work was so efficiently carried out that the building has received no further strengthening to this day.

Apart from its long history of wreck with accompanying loss of life, the Bishop appears to have been the scene of many other deaths, the rock once having been used for the execution of felons. This was in 1284, the twelfth year of the reign of Edward I, when 'John de Allet and Isabella his wife, hold the Isle of Scilly and hold there all kinds of pleas of the Crown throughout their jurisdiction and make indictments of felonies. When anyone is attained of a felony he ought to be taken to a certain rock in the sea, and with two barley loaves and one pitcher of water upon the same rock they leave the same felon, until by the flowing of the sea he is swallowed up'.[2]

The earliest recorded wreck on the Bishop itself is probably the brig *Theodorick*, from Mogodore to London, which struck in rough misty weather on 4 September 1839, whilst carrying general cargo. In the surrounding waters—the Bishop and Clerks to use an old expression—the earliest and best authenticated wreck is that of the *Royal Oak*, lost sometime during early 1665. The original document giving details of this wreck was unearthed in 1966 in the Bodleian Library, Oxford, and states 'The manner how ye ship Royall Oake,

Mr Robb Locke commander, from ye East Indies was cast away upon ye westerne rocks of Scilly called ye Bishopp and Clarks'. The ship had sailed from Bantam for England via Cape Bona Sprance and St Helena, and when forty leagues east of St Mary's was beset by gales. On the morning of 18 January, they 'were inviorned with rockes and beaches which terrible sight made us all bestire ourselves, some in ye toppes to see if there were any passage through but could fine none'. The report continues, telling us that the best bower anchor was dropped and the mainmast cut away, but this did not prevent the ship from being driven between two outcrops and foundering within fifteen minutes. Her crew reached some rocks but had to abandon them for higher ground when the tide rose. They remained there from early morning on the 18th until the 20th, not being rescued for fifty-two hours, 'where wee induced soe much cold yt all our leggs and hands were so swelled yt wee could but few of us stand.'[3]

A packet paddle-steamer was another early victim of the Bishop itself, the 600-ton *Brigand*, carrying 200 tons of bunker coal and patent fuel from Liverpool to London and St Petersburg. Valued at £3,200 she was a very fast vessel for her size, being fitted with a 200hp engine, and had been specially built for the Bristol-Liverpool trade. On Monday, 10 October 1842, the *Brigand* left Liverpool, her lookouts sighting St Agnes through rain and drizzle at 5 am on 12 October. Shortly afterwards, breakers were sighted ahead and she struck the Bishop Rock a mighty blow. Two large plates in her bow were stove in and, seconds later, she struck a second time broadside-on, so that the port paddle-wheel and box were driven bodily into the engine-room. A 5ft hole appeared in her side and the sea poured in, quickly swamping the boiler fires. Attempts were made to stem the inrush, but with such tremendous damage it was impossible, and on fast failing steam pressure the vessel drifted clear with one paddle-wheel still rotating. Fortunately, her construction was such that she had four watertight compartments and

continued to float. Firemen desperately shovelled coal overboard in an attempt to lighten her, whilst others manned the pumps, but inevitably the steam pressure failed completely, and with it all hope of ever reaching land. By 7 am her bows were under water and the twenty-seven crew took to the boats, only two of which were carried, so that both were dangerously overloaded. The *Brigand* finally sank in forty-five fathoms, seven miles from where she had first struck. Her master, Captain Hunt, and his crew landed at St Mary's safely and, after taking passage to Penzance in the pilot-boat *Antelope*, went overland to Hayle and shipped aboard the Cornish steamer *Herald* for Bristol.

In 1854, on 26 June, the Cardiff cutter *Belinda* struck the Bishop in thick fog. On passage from Cardiff to Cork with limestone, she got off again but took in water so fast that she foundered close at hand, her crew being saved. More fortunate was the Liverpool steamer, the *Castillian*, bound from Oporto to her home port with fruit and wine, which broke down off the Bishop when a piston-rod snapped on 13 September 1882 and would have drifted onto the rock but for the timely assistance of another vessel. Another lucky escape was that of the brigantine *Antares* of Nantes, found in distress just north of the lighthouse on 3 May 1890. Carrying pitwood from France to Llanelly, she was presumed to have struck the Crim and floated clear in the fog. It was a different story for the Swedish barque *Sultana* which went to the bottom on Sunday, 17 February 1895. She had become unmanageable after springing a leak and was abandoned close to the Bishop light, her eighteen crew landing at Scilly from a French schooner.

There was one wreck that struck the lighthouse itself; that was on 22 June 1901 at 7.30 pm, when the four-masted Liverpool barque *Falkland*, Capt. Gracie, 135 days out from Tacoma with grain, Puget Sound to Falmouth for orders, was carried on to the rocks during a strong south-westerly gale after missing stays. She struck broadside-on, her mainyard striking the light tower, and after drifting half a mile to the north, fell on to her beam ends and sank.

The Liverpool barque *Falkland* actually struck the Bishop Rock Lighthouse with her mainyard on 22 June 1901, before drifting some half a mile north and sinking.

Twenty-five of the crew, along with Mrs Gracie and her child, escaped in the port boat, the captain and five others remaining on board to launch the starboard boat, jammed on its skids. Eventually the boat fell out of its stowage and the captain led the others over the now horizontal jiggermast to reach it. At that moment compressed air blew out the charthouse roof, and the *Falkland*, deprived of her buoyancy, went down like a stone. Captain Gracie and the mate were sucked down and drowned, the mate's body coming ashore in Hell Bay, whilst one of the seamen, known only as 'old George', slipped from his lifebelt and drowned, as did the steward and two able seamen. Built in 1889 by W. H. Potter & Sons for the Palace Shipping Co Ltd, the *Falkland*, 2,867 tons gross, was sister-ship to the *Holinwood*, lost by fire in the late 1890s.

On 11 July 1921, the Bishop lighthouse-keepers were afforded a grandstand view of the destruction by fire of the steamer *Western Front*, Jacksonville to London, carrying 7,000 tons of naval stores which included naphtha, turpentine and resin, a highly inflammable combination of materials. Registered at Seattle, the 5,695 tons gross steamer had been built in 1917 for the US Shipping Board by the Skinner, Eddy Corporation. Fire was discovered on board when some twenty miles west of the Bishop, but by the time the St Mary's lifeboat *Elsie* had reached the scene and rescued forty of the crew from their own boats, the *Western Front* had drifted to within seven miles of the Western Rocks. The steamer *British Earl* saved the rest of the crew, the only casualty being one able seamen. During the First and Second World Wars there were many tragic

The burnt out hull of the American SS *Western Front*, after she caught fire carrying a cargo of naphtha, resin and turpentine, SW of the Bishop Rock, 11 July 1921.

losses in the vicinity of the Bishop, some of which are mentioned in Chapter 8, but the only inshore incident concerned the German submarine U-681 which is thought to have struck either the Bishop or Crebinicks on 11 March 1945. Badly damaged, she tried to reach a neutral port in Ireland, but was sighted and attacked by an American Liberator aircraft, whereupon she was scuttled and abandoned by her crew.

East of the Bishop lie the Crebinicks and the Retarrier Ledges, and the Ledges were much in the headlines of British and American newspapers in 1875 when, on 7 May, they were struck by the 3,421 tons gross passenger-steamer *Schiller* of Hamburg, which sank with the loss of 311 lives. The Western Rocks were blanketed in dense fog that night, the worst in living

memory, as this German Transatlantic Steam Navigation liner crept towards the Isles of Scilly. By 8 o'clock that evening Capt. Thomas had reduced speed to four knots and posted double lookouts. An hour later, with the Bishop still neither seen nor heard, volunteers from amongst the male passengers were asked to act as additional lookouts, with the promise of a bottle of champagne to the first man to see the light, or hear the Bishop Rock fog bell. The prize was never collected, for just before ten o'clock the liner struck the Retarriers, having passed inside of the lighthouse. Her engines pulled her clear of the rocks, but three huge waves in succession struck her beam-on, and the stricken vessel was flung broadside on to the reef. Rockets and signal-guns were fired — some of the witnesses later gave their number as at least ten — but these were mistaken by the lighthouse-keepers and islanders alike as a vessel signalling her arrival off Scilly, as was the custom. Pandemonium broke out on deck amongst the fear-crazed passengers and the captain was obliged to fire a revolver over their heads to retain some order, but there was little hope for anyone. The *Schiller* carried only eight boats, two of which were reduced to match-wood when one of her funnels collapsed across them. Two others jammed in their chocks due to the ship's heavy list, one capsized as soon as it touched the sea and another smashed against the hull in lowering and hung useless from its davits. Only two boats finally got clear and drifted off into the gloom of the night. For the 320 men, women and children left aboard that night, it was to be one of mounting horror. The sea boomed all around them, fog closed in from all sides, and they had not the slightest idea where they were or what hope there was of rescue.

By midnight the *Schiller* had assumed an even heavier list, and Capt. Thomas ordered the women and children to gather on the deckhouse roof, over the midships saloon. Fifty of them huddled there, weeping mothers and bewildered youngsters, momentarily clear of the seas which swept the length of the flush-decked vessel. Then another succession of giant seas struck the wreck, the first tearing off the roof of the deckhouse, the second hurling it and its occupants into the sea. By the time the third had passed, not one of those who had been clinging to the deckhouse was to be seen. At dawn, a Sennen fishing-boat was first on the scene and rescued seven men, two of whom later died from exposure. Soon a whole fleet of small boats, accompanied by the packet steamer *Lady of the Isles*, appeared. During the morning, two men were rescued from off rocks, and the two lifeboats from the wreck landed at Tresco with twenty-six men and one woman aboard. Of the *Schiller's* original complement of fifty-nine saloon, seventy-five second class and one hundred and twenty steerage-class passengers, plus one hundred and one crew, a total of 355, only forty-two men and one woman survived.

The *Schiller* had left New York for Hamburg via Plymouth on 27 April, carrying 250 bags of Australian and New Zealand mail, a valuable

An artists impression of the German liner *Schiller*, lost on Retarrier Ledges, close to the Bishop Rock, 7 May 1875, with the loss of 311 lives.

general cargo, and £60,000 in American twenty-dollar gold pieces, 300,000 coins in all. Sometime after she was wrecked, the sea ripped the ship open and the specie fell down amongst the wreckage. The mail-bags floated up and out on the tide, thirty being found ashore on Samson and others as far away as Penzance. Three days after the wreck, on Monday, 10 May, the *Queen of the Bay* left the mainland for St Mary's, and between the Longships and Wolf Rock sailed through a sea of wreckage consisting of light woodwork, empty barrels, cigar boxes, cases, tables, portions of agricultural implements, mail-bags, and one male corpse, still wearing a lifebelt and with $135 in his pockets.

Weather conditions were so bad that no one could approach the wreck to carry out salvage or a survey until 11 May, when the ship was found in five fathoms, only two spars showing above the surface. The first divers went down on the 15th and found the vessel smashed to pieces, with no signs of the bullion. After two hours underwater, they surfaced with only two sewing machines ! The coin had been shipped in six small kegs, the size of small herring barrels, each containing 50,000 gold pieces. The casks, marked 'F.S.B. & Co.', had been stowed amidships between the main and spar decks, but it was soon apparent that it was going to be no easy task to find them, and that a full-scale salvage operation would be necessary. Meanwhile, bodies were being landed at St Mary's and needed immediate attention. Thirty-seven interments took place on the Monday following the wreck, twenty the following day, and ninety on Thursday. Their burial presented something of a problem, and those which were not embalmed and sent to America were laid to rest in plain deal boxes painted black. Mass graves were dug in the Old Town churchyard, rock having to be blasted in order to make sufficient room. With no hearse on the island, pony carts with two coffins on each were used. and the whole of the Scilly population went into mourning. To quote an account from the *Sherborne Mercury* newspaper, 'the most melancholy spectacle that ever was,

or we trust will never be seen again, passed through Helston to St Keverne on Tuesday, 24 May, being several wagons laden with coffins to the amount of fifty.'[4] Why the coffins were reported as being en route to St Keverne is something of a mystery.

It was not until 11 August that the first coin was found, after which large numbers were seen scattered loose around the engine-room. On Friday, 20 August, 561 gold pieces were salvaged, 848 on Saturday and 108 on Monday, so that by the end of August £6,068 had been salvaged. Work continued until 6 May, 1876, by which time the divers had recovered a total of £57,712 out of a possible £60,000. They literally took the wreck to pieces, searching not only for the gold pieces but for valuables lost by the passengers. One American passenger, a Mr Kornblum, a paper manufacturer from New York, had on board with him eighty-five gold watches, a large quantity of diamond jewellery and £500 in coin. Items of the *Schiller's* general cargo, such as bags of feathers, casks of resin, flour etc, were picked up all round Cornwall for weeks afterwards. Built by Napiers of Glasgow for Alexander Stephens (Shipbuilders), the *Schiller* had been launched in August 1873, and was on her last voyage for her current owners before being incorporated in the Eagle Line. In Old Town churchyard, St Mary's, a simple stone monument is engraved. 'In memory of Louise Holzmaister, born at New York, 15 May 1851, who lost her life in the wreck of the ss *Schiller* on the Scilly Isles, 7 May 1875. Her body rests in the deep, this monument has been erected to her memory as a mark of affection by a sorrowing husband'. Close at hand are the graves of two other victims.

Tragic disaster though it was, the wreck of the *Schiller* was by no means the worst amongst the Western Rocks, for the greatest maritime disaster England has known occurred less than half a mile away from the Retarriers, on Gilstone Reef. Here, on 22 October 1707, Admiral Sir Clowdisley Shovell and some 1,628 officers and men of the Royal Navy met their deaths when HMS *Association, Eagle,*

Romney and *Firebrand* all struck within the same area and went down. Technically, only the *Association* was lost on the Gilstone, the *Eagle* being lost on either Tearing Ledge, or the Crim, the *Firebrand* close to Menglow near St Agnes, and the *Romney* has never been found, but for ease of narration they can be considered as one area. Returning to Portsmouth after a successful campaign in the Mediterranean, these ships were part of a fleet of twenty-one vessels, nine of which were of seventy guns or more. They left Gibraltar on 27 September 1707, but a week later, after encountering gales from all points of the compass, they were hopelessly lost. So much so that the fleet hove to in order to take soundings with their deep-leads, which caused them to believe they were due west of Ushant, and that the English Channel lay open before them. Legend has it that a meeting of sailing masters took place on board the flagship, and that only Sir William Jumper of the *Lennox* disagreed with the others regarding their position, insisting they would sight Scilly within three hours – but no such meeting took place. The fleet sailed on, only now the *Royal Anne*, *Panther* and *Firebrand* were leading and the three columns of ships, *Le Valeur*, *Lennox* and *Phoenix* having been despatched to Falmouth to escort a merchant navy convoy up Channel to the Thames.

The great ships lumbered on, all unaware of the dangers that lay ahead. At about 8 o'clock on the evening of 22 October, the flagship plunged straight on to the Gilstone Ledges and sank almost immediately at high water with her entire crew of some 650. She was followed closely by the others, and in quick succession the *Eagle*, *Romney* and *Firebrand* all struck and went under. The *St George*, Captain Dursley, 90 guns, was exceptionally fortunate in that she struck the Gilstone but floated clear with little damage other than a smashed stern gallery. Unknown to the fleet, the lead ships despatched earlier in the day had also encountered the Western Rocks, leaving the *Phoenix* badly damaged and full of water in New Grimsby harbour, Tresco, where she was to remain for almost four months. Of the 1,673

men aboard the wrecked ships, only twenty-six survivors were reported, twenty-five from the *Firebrand*, and a quarter-master, George Lawrence from the *Romney*. There may, in fact, have been others, since the majority of men in service were 'pressed' and would probably have seized such a heaven-sent opportunity to desert, although the advantages of desertion on eighteenth-century Scilly are doubtful and hanging would have been their punishment if caught.

The body of Sir Clowdisley was found washed ashore at Porth Hellick, a sandy bay on the south side of St Mary's, about seven miles from the scene of the wrecks. He was said to have been alive when found, and murdered for the valuable rings he wore, his hands being mutilated in order to remove the jewellery, after which the naked body was buried on the foreshore. Later, he was exhumed, identified, and taken to Westminster where Queen Anne ordered a state funeral. Legend has it that many years after the incident, a St Mary's woman made a death-bed confession to the crime and produced one of the rings, set with a fine emerald and diamonds. Another more credible version states that a soldier found the body and removed the rings. When Lady Clowdisley enquired as to their whereabouts, they were handed over, in return for which both he and his wife received a pension for life. The whole story of Sir Clowdisley's supposed murder after coming ashore in one of the ship's boats is highly questionable, and it is more likely that he was washed ashore, already drowned, along with flotsam which, by coincidence, included boat timbers. A letter still in existence states that after his body was exhumed it was found, 'his ring was lost from his finger, which last however left the impression on his finger as also a second. His head was not at all swelled with the water, neither had he any bruises nor scars upon him, save for a small scratch over one eye as if by a pin'.[5]

Overleaf: An early lithograph depicting the loss of the warships *Association* and *Eagle* amongst the Western Rocks, 22 October 1707.

There was great activity on the Gilstone after the wrecks and this no doubt continued for several years, producing the richest harvest the islanders have ever enjoyed. It is now known that the wreck of the *Association* went to pieces in a very short time, but parts of the ship must have shown at low water. Certainly the most attractive area of the ship, the poop, with its valuable plate and personal effects, would have been readily accessible, and salvage work, even on such an exposed site, was perfectly feasible 260 years ago. It is known that several brass and iron guns were recovered, along with anchors, using diving bells, together with a great deal of specie and plate that went unrecorded. A recent book about the *Association* published in 1985 has revealed to a certain extent, why the flagship was carrying such a vast wealth in specie. Much of this would have been the residue of funds to support the Toulon siege, plus the regimental funds of the Coldstream Guards, and possibly gold belonging to Portuguese bankers.

A large-scale salvage attempt was made on behalf of the Admiralty by Deputy-Paymaster Herbert in 1709/10, who ordered a base camp set up for the purpose on Rosevear, and the wreck was again visited in 1852 by men working on the Bishop lighthouse, and yet again in 1875 by divers recovering gold from the *Schiller*. Fittingly, the wreck site was then relocated by divers of the modern navy in 1967, after intensive research and underwater surveys spread out over four years. Since then, the site has yielded ten bronze cannon of varying sizes from 2 tons upwards, 28-pounders down to miniature, almost toy, signal-guns weighing only 50 lb or so. Other artefacts have included silver spurs, gold 'posy' rings, uniform buttons, eating and table utensils, human bones, candlesticks, lead inkwells, dividers, and, of course coins, both gold and silver. Exactly how many will never be known for the salvage laws of Great Britain do not encourage honesty.

In 1969, one of the many civilian diving teams located a cannon site in deep water off Tearing Ledge, recovering a large ship's bell bearing a broad arrow mark and the date 1701, as well as a navigational slate and artefacts.

According to the Gostelo map in the British Library, which purports to show the location of all four ships lost in the 1707 disaster, this is where the *Romney* sank, with the *Eagle* somewhere on the Crim. However, there is good reason, based on the number of cannon and their sizes, to speculate that the two sites may have been incorrectly identified at the time, when only their topmasts showed above the surface; a genuine mistake compounded by this quaint and historic map. If so, then the wreck on Tearing Ledge could well be the *Eagle*, but either way, the site of the third largest warship in the 1707 disaster has yet to be identified. A cannon site with some 30 guns which lie in 135 ft (41m) of water close to Zantman's rock, on the seaward side of the Crim, from which a small bell and artefacts have been recovered may well be one of the East Indiamen wrecked amongst the Western rocks. 1969 also saw the recovery of a unique bronze cannon from the *Association* site. Recovered from beneath a boulder weighing at least 100 tons, this gun carries an inscription which, loosely translated, reads, 'Charles of Devonia ordered this gun made by Thomas Pitt in the year 1604'. It was a great pity that neither the Isles of Scilly nor the National Maritime Museum were able to retain a cross-section of the items found for permanent exhibition, for now, following two public auctions of the artefacts and coins, one would have to travel to the four corners of the earth to see them all.

Sir Clowdisley's ships were not the only losses in and around the Gilstone area; a large unidentified sailing vessel was lost here in 1750, and a tobacco-laden Virginian on 7 June 1788. The 347-ton barque *John Esdaile* of North Shields, from Green Island to London,

A superb example of early 17th century gunfounding; a bronze gun salvaged from the wreck site of the *Association* in 1969. The inscription in Latin, reads:

"Charles Earl of Devonshire and Master of Ordnance commissioned Thomas Pitt the maker, year 1604"

This gun, a falconetter, valued at over £20,000, is on public display in the Isles of Scilly museum.

Early finds from the wreck site of HM man o'war *Association* are examined in the Queens Warehouse, St. Mary's, by the Receiver of Wreck, Customs Officer 'Bill' Saunby, July 1967. Bronze pulley sheaves stand alongside a 3 ton bronze cannon, with smaller bronze guns, sounding leads, and other artefact material.

also struck on the Gilstone Ledges on 1 December 1845, but despite being towed into Smith Sound, went to pieces a week later. Her cargo of deals was salvaged from the beaches of Annet and St Agnes, and all her crew were saved, unlike the unfortunate Greeks aboard the steamer *Antonios* wrecked on Old Bess in early December 1912. The first local knowledge of this wreck came when pieces of lifeboat, derricks, hatch covers and literally thousands of oranges were washed ashore on St Agnes three days later. Only one body was ever found, badly disfigured by the sea, and remains unnamed. An oar blade marked *Greta Holme* led to identification, proving the vessel to be the 2,626-ton steamer *Antonios* of Andros, Greece, ex-*Greta Holme*. Built in 1894 by J. L.

Thompson of Sunderland, she was on passage from Fiume to Liverpool, having left Algiers on 2 December. The last shipping loss of any significance amongst the Western rocks probably took place on 13 February 1977, in bad visibility and heavy weather on Pednathise. The St Mary's lifeboat was launched at 0215hrs on 14 February, to search for the French trawler *Enfant de Bretagne* of St Malo. By the light of a parachute flare, the crew of the lifeboat eventually saw the bow of the wreck, and heard voices shouting, but then the wreckage disappeared. A navy helicopter from RNAS Culdrose later recovered one body, the lifeboat a second, divers confirming the identity of the wreck from which there were no survivors.

Swinging north from the Gilstone and Pednathise, there lies a semi-circle of rocks which is a natural trap for east-bound ships. Starting at the southern end, they are Daisy, Rosevean, Rosevear, Jackys Rock, Crebawethan and their associated Santasperry Neck and Brow-of-Ponds. The three earliest wrecks on

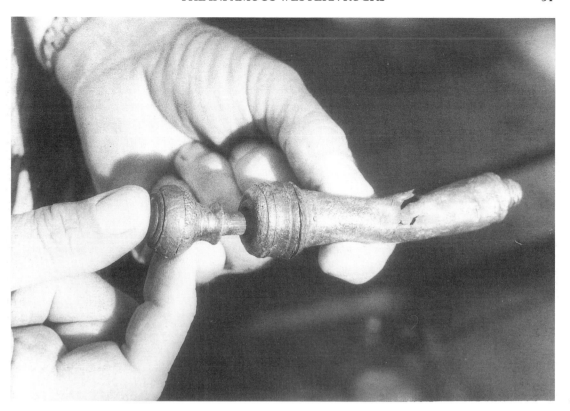

A pewter medical syringe, probably part of the surgeon's chest carried on board the *Association*, recovered by divers in 1968.

Rosevean, which occurred in 1730, 1752 and 1762, cannot now be identified since their names are not recorded, although some details are known. The first of these was a ship laden with wine from the Canary Islands, whose master, Capt. Roberts, at first refused to leave his vessel because of a large sum of money on board. A worsening of the weather eventually forced him to abandon his ship and, after reaching Rosevean, he and another survivor remained lashed to a rock for three days before rescue. The wreck in 1752 was that of a Dutchman carrying cotton from Smyrna, and from this there were no survivors, unlike the French vessel lost in 1762 from which six of the crew escaped by clinging to floating timbers, although twelve others drowned. At midnight on 26 February 1784, the same night that a transport vessel from New York came in at the back of Bryher in a south-west gale and was nearly wrecked, the East Indies packet *Nancy* struck first on Gilstone and then drove ashore on Rosevear. Her passengers were mostly army

officers returning from Madras, but there was one woman on board, an actress named Mrs Cargill, who carried a small fortune in cash with her. A local pilot-boat eventually reached the wreck, and the bodies of the actress and two men were removed to St Mary's for burial, but others were far gone in putrefaction and were left to the sea. Mail from the wreck was salvaged and sent to London, but little or no cargo was recovered.

The sloop *Mary* of Fishguard was equally unlucky, being wrecked on 20 March 1819, with a cargo of oats from Youghall to Southampton, whilst thick fog caused the loss of the Plymouth schooner *Solace* from Lisbon, Barrett master, on 27 April 1839. She struck a shallow reef and went to pieces the following day in a ground swell, but her crew of five managed to save their personal belongings before taking to the boats. Another Dutch owned vessel lost in the area was the *Nickerie*, a barque, registered at Rotterdam, Haweg master. On passage from Samarang in Batavia to her home port with coffee and sugar, she struck a rock south-west of Rosevear during the night of 21 November 1843 when, in fact, her captain thought he was well up the English Channel. She was got off, but struck again only ten minutes later and almost went to pieces. Eight of the crew drowned, including the chief officer and doctor, the eleven men remaining having to cling to wreckage until daybreak. They then attempted to construct a raft but were unable to remove sufficient timber from the wreck, and the bo'sun died trying to swim a line ashore. Sometime later the ship's carpenter died from exposure, and although the rest reached Rosevear, only two survived long enough to be rescued.

In 1925, two steam trawlers went ashore on Rosevear, although only one was actually wrecked on the island. The first stranding occurred at midnight on 21 March 1925, and the lookouts on board the French *Cité de Verdun* caught only a brief glimpse of the Bishop light through a blinding snowstorm before their ship struck the rocks. Her crew of thirty got ashore, built a shelter and lit a fire before sending up signals of distress, in answer to which the St Mary's lifeboat *Elsie*, coxswain Lethbridge, went out amongst the Western Rocks and within forty-five minutes had them all safely aboard. The RNLI crew responsible for their rescue later received awards from the French government, and amongst the many souvenirs of the wreck which found their way to St Mary's were the ship's nameboards, which can still be seen in the Atlantic and Mermaid inns. The second incident concerned another French trawler, the *Europe* of Boulogne, which went ashore during fog at 2.42 am on 12 June in almost exactly the same spot as the *Cité de Verdun*. A coastguard on St Mary's spotted her distress flares and alerted the lifeboat crew but, as their boat was laid up at the time for repairs, privately-owned craft went out to search west of Annet. They found the 119-ton steam

trawler stranded on the rocks with only her captain and four men aboard, the remainder having already taken to the boats which now lay some distance off. They were convinced that the *Europe* was doomed and were waiting for her to sink. As the tide rose, so the trawler was worked off the rocks, her crew re-embarked, and at 5.15 am she radioed Land's End that she was clear and making for Dunkirk, only slightly damaged.

The Western Rocks have witnessed so many tragedies that their individual enormity, although dreadful at the time, soon tend to be forgotten or overshadowed. A total of seven East Indiamen have found themselves in difficulties in the Scillies, all in this quarter of the islands, only one of which, unfortunately the smallest and least valuable, was saved. This was the *Supply*, an English Company pinnace homeward bound from Bantam with despatches, which went ashore in 1617. Less fortunate was the EIC *Phoenix* of 450 tons, homeward bound with a valuable cargo of white pepper in bags, and cloth, which was lost somewhere amongst the Western rocks on 11 January 1680. Armed with 30 guns, under Captain Wildy, on her fourth voyage to the east, her lading was valued at £10,177.18s. Much of the pepper and textiles were sold on Scilly, a Thomas Abney paying '£202.8s.1d for 269 pieces of Peerlongs', but these sums were minuscule compared to the value of the 'treasure' – presumably all silver specie, which went down on board the Dutch VOC (Verenidge Oostindische Compagnie) ship *Prinses Maria* in February 1686. She sank in shallow water close to Silver Carn, just north of Santaspery Neck, very close to where the SS *Thames* was lost 155 years later. Carrying 46 guns, the value of silver was so great that James I sent down his personal yacht, retainers and soldiers, to recover as much as they could for the king's coffers. Relocated in 1973 under deep sand by a diving team led by Rex Cowan, the site yielded numerous artefacts, a small quantity of reale coins, iron cannon and timbers, but had obviously been heavily salvaged at the time she sank. One particularly tragic wreck, thought to be the earliest steamer lost at Scilly, was the 500-ton steamer *Thames* on 4 January 1841. Owned by the City of Dublin Steam Packet Co, the 14-year-old vessel left the Liffy for London on 2 January with 36 passengers, of whom some 30 were young recruits for the British Army and 26 crew. Early on 4 January, while battling against a full westerly gale accompanied by rain squalls, snow and thunder, one particularly heavy sea came aboard, flooding the hold, cabins and boiler-room and putting out the fires. Almost simultaneously breakers were sighted to leeward, and Captain Grey ordered sail to be set on the main and foremasts in an attempt to work her clear but, waterlogged and helpless, the little *Thames* fell broadside onto Jackys Rock, between Rosevear and Crebawethan. A worse situation for those on board could hardly be envisaged as seas swept the upper deck, the steamer surrounded by rocks on all sides and illuminated only by flashes of lightning. Distress flares were burnt but went unseen by those on shore, and it was not until daybreak that the first islanders noticed the wreck. Ten of them put out in the gig *Thomas*, followed by the *Bee*, and the *Briton*, the pilot-cutter *Active* and the St Mary's lifeboat which, incidentally, did not then have a name.

The gig *Thomas* was the first to reach the wreck, by now lying with her bows under water and with the survivors crowded on to her small poop. Female passengers were the first to be taken off, a distraught and near-hysterical Celia Morris having to be forcibly pulled from her father's arms. A wave then filled the little gig almost level with her gunwales and while half the crew bailed furiously, the others pulled Mary Meyler and Mary Gregory, both stewardesses, through the sea on a line to safety. With her crew still bailing, the gig was then rowed to Gorregon, where the three women, in desperate straits, were transferred to the *Active*. The gale then shifted into the east, and prevented any further boats from reaching the *Thames*, by now surrounded by huge seas and almost engulfed in the breaking water. Meanwhile, on board the cutter *Active*, all three

women, suffering from exposure but alive, were landed at St Agnes. The Irish recruits attempted to save themselves by launching a lifeboat, but it quickly filled and sank, as did a second. Five of the steamer's crew then managed to construct a raft but, once in the sea, it soon capsized and was later thrown ashore on Rosevear, only one of the five reaching safety. Alone on the rock, he searched the foreshore, calling out in the hope of finding others alive, but found only useless wreckage and a barrel of porter. This he pulled to higher ground, broached, and drank some of the contents, after which he emptied it, lined it with grass, and climbed inside to fall asleep in his improvised shelter. A search party found him the following day, still asleep and, along with bodies recovered from the sea, he was brought to St Mary's. Sixty lives, including Capt Grey, were lost in the wreck of the *Thames*, one of the worst disasters amongst the islands. Six weeks after the wreck during a period of fine weather, Deane's diving apparatus, the forerunner of all helmet-diving equipment, was employed on the *Thames* and her anchor cables were salvaged during the first day's work.

Behind Rosevear and Jackys Rock, to the east, is an area known locally as the Brow-of-Ponds, which was the scene of two wrecks, those of an Austrian brig and a steamer. The brig *Aurora* went ashore at 2 am on 19 August 1860, while carrying wheat from Ibrail for Falmouth. Capt. Alessio Merlato and his crew got away in the ship's boat only with great difficulty, finally landing at St Mary's. Little of her cargo and only a few spars were saved, and the wreck itself was sold on 23 August. Poor visibility due to fog sent the *Aurora* ashore, and exactly the same conditions caused the wreck of the steamer *Sado* of London some ten years later on 20 April 1870. She had left Oporto for Liverpool on the 17th with a general cargo of wine, wool, oranges, minerals, eggs and 30 bullocks, and all was well until a little after midnight on the 20th when fog was encountered. The *Sado*, however, continued at full speed, about nine knots, until 2.40 am, when the second mate saw broken water ahead. Her helm was put hard over, but more rocks appeared ahead and even as her engines were put full astern she struck. The 325-ton vessel became a total loss and at the enquiry her master, Captain R. Hoodless, had his certificate suspended for three months for not using the sounding lead, and for failing to reduce speed in fog.

Crebawethan, north of Jackys Rock, has claimed at least seven ships, one of the earliest being the *Amelia* of London on 1 September 1810. Bound from Demerara with rum, coffee, cotton and sugar for London, she went ashore and was abandoned to the sea along with her cargo, one box of silver and another of American dollars. A St Ives schooner, the *Minerva*, Hicks master, was also lost here on 13 October 1836 with only one survivor, and another victim of nearby Round rock was the 200 ton Liverpool schooner, *Douro*, Gowland Master, on 27 January 1843. Bound from Liverpool to Oporto with a cargo described as 'baled goods, armoury and brass stops', she struck and sank in fog, her entire crew being lost. Six bodies and the ship's figurehead were later recovered, but little else. When located by divers accidentally in the early 1970's, the 'brass stops' in her cargo proved to be thousands of brass manillas, bracelet-type tokens used in the West African slave trade, but there is no proof that the *Douro* was herself engaged in the slave trade.

Two pounds per head was the price offered for every live steer landed on Annet from the wreck of the Liverpool steamer *Castleford* on 8 June 1887. This 3,044 tons gross vessel, launched at Sunderland in 1883 for the Sunderland S.B. Co, had left Montreal for the Thames on 27 May, carrying a general cargo, 450 prime steers on deck, eighteen cattlemen, one passenger and thirty-two crew. Dense fog around the Scillies forced Capt. McLean to reduce speed upon approaching the islands, and when a sounding showed fifty-six fathoms the ship's engines were stopped in order to listen for the Bishop fog-signal. While the captain was in the chartroom attempting to work out his position, the chief officer ordered the engines to ahead again, and before the captain could regain the bridge to countermand the order the *Castleford* was aground on the Crebawethan. Both Nos 1 and 2 holds flooded and when the boiler-room bulkhead collapsed, flooding the engine-room, her crew abandoned ship. During the subsequent salvage work, cattle were roped by the horns to gigs, which towed them to Annet where they roamed around for ten days before being shipped to Falmouth. Many of the beasts drowned, and two local gigs fell victims to the animals; the *Gipsy* was holed by the horns of one frantic animal and the *O & M* had her bows smashed when a steer fell on to her from the deck of the wreck. The *Castleford* finally broke in two forward of the bridge on 19 July and dead steers were washed out of the holds, some reaching Lelant and Penzance, on the mainland.

Eleven years later, on 26 May 1898, a small Newlyn fishing lugger, the *Nyanza*, skippered by Alfred Richards, struck the Crims and sprung such a serious leak that she had to be run ashore on Gt Crebawethan. The St Agnes lifeboat, *James and Caroline*, was able to save four of her crew and some of the fishing gear, while an island boat saved a fifth man, but nothing could be done about the lugger, which went to pieces where she lay. An armed auxiliary naval trawler, HMS *Carbineer*, was the last victim of Crebawethan, having struck the Crim on 18 May 1916. A Scillonian crew member, W. Trenear, knowing the waters, advised the captain to run her ashore on Crebawethan where she became a total loss, rather than have her sink in the deep waters of Broad Sound.

Reference has already been made to the Crim, the most seaward of the Western Rocks and an extremely dangerous reef which has terminated the career of something like thirty vessels. In 1782, an unidentified Venetian ship was wrecked here while carrying Castille soap, wine, almonds and oil from Marseilles to London. Eleven of her crew saved themselves by clinging to a mast, which carried them to New Grimsby, Tresco. A French barque, the *Osirus*, was lost on 29 May 1838 during an easterly gale, also the Glasgow schooner *Eagle*, which struck first on the Crim in fog on 18 January 1848, then several other rocks, and finally the Bishop before sinking. She was bound from her home port to Charante with iron and coal, and Capt Scott and his crew had a narrow escape when the mainyard fell while they were abandoning ship and almost sank their longboat. Another victim of the Crim was the Neopolitan brig *San Giorgio* which, badly damaged by storm, drifted onto the reef on 14 September 1851, floated clear and then fell on her side, slowly sinking. Cries for help from the crew were answered by the schooner *Galway Ark*, which took them off and landed them at St Mary's within an hour of the incident. The wreck then drifted out to sea and was later found sixty miles offshore. It took the combined efforts of fifteen pilot-cutters and a schooner to get the brig back to Scilly, where her entire cargo of wood and olive oil was saved. The salvors received £2,000 for the cargo, and £110 for the vessel's hull, and after being repaired locally at a St Mary's shipyard, the brig sailed again as the *Lion* of Scilly.

The first of many such large sailing vessels to fall foul of the Crim was the Liverpool full-rigger *Custos*, lost on 28 August 1856. With a cargo of rum, brandy, soap and gunpowder, she sank within ten minutes, only a small quantity of soap and eighty casks of spirit being salvaged. *Good Intent*, a brigantine loaded with coal, hit the Crim and sank in the December of 1867, whilst the barque *Gloria* of Genoa, after hitting the reef on 26 August 1875, managed to stagger on to St Mary's, assisted by the *Lady of the Isles*, where her cargo of ore and grass from Pomeron was saved. When the Liverpool steamer *Culmore* of 540 tons gross hit the rocks in fog on 7 May 1881, she went down so quickly that Capt Coble, the chief and second engineers, and a steward went down with her, although the captain and steward surfaced only to die aboard a small boat sometime later. After striking, her cargo spewed out across the width of the Western Rocks, and Valencia oranges, pepper and onions came ashore throughout the

After striking the Crim Rocks at the northern end on 18 June 1909, the French steel ship *Leon Bureau* tore a hole in her bow, and drifted off into the fog. Her crew managed to sail her all the way to Falmouth where she was beached and saved.

Scillies. Owned by Edward Paul of Liverpool, the *Culmore* was reported as sinking in deep water, beyond hope of salvage. Although the *Indipendenza*, a Genoan barque was lost as a result of hitting the Crim on 24 September 1881, she finally sank on the rocks overlooked by Star Castle, St Mary's, so that her story has been included in Chapter 4.

Next of the big full-riggers to fall foul of the area was the steel-hulled, 1,765-ton *Leon Bureau* of Nantes, carrying 2,600 tons of wheat from Adelaide to Falmouth. On 18 June 1909 she hit the northern end of the rocks, tore a large hole in her bow and drifted off into the fog, the crew only just managing to hold their own with the pumps. Two naval torpedo-boats were sighted close to the Seven Stones reef, but both failed to see the *Leon Bureau's* signals of distress, and it was not until she entered Mount's Bay that a Trinity pilot at Newlyn noticed her plight. Even then the pilot-gig was unable to catch up with the Frenchman until

off Mullion, by which time there was six feet of water in the holds. Tugs came to her assistance, and at 5.15 pm the *Leon Bureau* was beached alongside the eastern extension pier at Falmouth. It was the end of a somewhat disastrous voyage. When off Cape Horn in March the sea had swept away the ship's binnacle, wheel, rudder, bell and topgallant yard, in addition to breaking the bosun's leg. The following month Francis Allard, the ship's boy, had fallen from a yard and died, and only hours before the ship struck the Crim an able seaman had fallen over the poop deck rail and fractured his ribs. The final incident occurred whilst alongside at Falmouth, when the bow anchor slipped while being catted and crushed a seaman's foot.

Although the *Ardencraig* of Glasgow did not actually hit the Crim, she missed them by only yards and carried on to strike the Gunners, another dangerous shelf about a mile and a half to the east. Her wreck was signalled by the boom of the Bishop gun, which brought out the *Charles Deere James* and *Henry Dundas* lifeboats from St Agnes and St Mary's on 8 January 1911. Thirty minutes later they had found the

The full-rigged iron ship *Ardencraig* half full of water and wallowing in Broad Sound, 8 January 1911, after striking the Gunners, a dangerous reef. She capsized and sank shortly after this photograph was taken.

huge three-master wallowing in the swell of North Channel, her foreyards aback. Shortly afterwards, she rolled over and sank bows first in deep water. The *Ardencraig* was one hundred days out from Melbourne with wheat for Calais via Queenstown for orders, and had, in fact, left Ireland the previous day. Whilst Capt. Dunning was at dinner, convinced that his ship was safely to the south-west of the Bishop, she ran onto the Gunners. Although the crew of thirty-one were all saved either in their own boats or by the Scilly lifeboats, a court of enquiry found the captain guilty of improper navigation and unseamanlike behaviour and suspended his master's certificate for three months. The ship had been built in 1886 by Russell & Co of Greenock for the Port Line Ltd.

Two Cape Horners fell victim to the Crim during the latter part of 1913, the same year in which both the *Cromdale* and the *Queen Margaret* were lost on the Lizard. Bound from Iquique to Falmouth with nitrate, the 1,975 gross tons *Susanna*, a ship of Hamburg, was sailing in dense fog on 14 August when her lookouts heard the Bishop minute-gun, but were unable to determine the precise direction from which the sound was coming. A few minutes later she struck heavily on the southern side of Zantmans Rock and commenced to fill. After the ship's boats had been lowered, the crew remained aboard to see if she could be saved, but by midnight there were signs of breaking up and she was abandoned. No sooner had the last of the twenty-two crew taken to the boats than the *Susanna* rolled over, broke in two and foundered. The wreck still lies close to the south-western side of Zantmans, in 90ft of water, reduced to unrecognisable scrap metal by ground seas. When visited in 1968 by the author, only pieces of broken china marked 'Villeroy and Boch. Dresden' could identify the vessel, but since then the ship's bell has been located and raised.

The second loss on the Crim that same year was the Glasgow ship *Thornliebank* of 2,105 tons gross. On her outward voyage she had carried a cargo of coal from Port Talbot to Iquique and had then gone on to Pisagua, in Chile, where she loaded a home cargo of salt-petre worth £30,000. Nearing home and heading for Falmouth for orders, she ran into fog off the Scillies, but it cleared sufficiently for the deck watch to recognise the Round Island light and when they thought they had also identified the Bishop, the master set a course due sw. At 5 am the following morning, 28 November, just as the port watch was tacking ship, there was a grating rumble, the vessel brought up sharply and began to roll heavily. She assumed a heavy list to starboard, so that only the boats on that side could be lowered, and less than five minutes later fell on her side until the topsail yards touched the sea, then rolled right over and sank, less than 150yd from the wreck of the *Susanna*. Her crew of twenty-five, having watched their ship go down from the comparative safety of their boats, then rowed towards the Bishop, where they saw one of the keepers on the gallery but for some reason were unable to attract his attention. They then decided to row on to St Agnes, but were met off Melledgan by the lifeboat *Charles Deere James* and escorted into St Mary's. Later, wreckage from the vessel, a cork lifebelt and a nameboard, came ashore on the north coast of Cornwall, between Perranporth and Watergate Bay. The 2,105-ton *Thornliebank* was the last sailing ship built for the Bank Line Ltd (A. Weir and Co of Glasgow), having been launched by Russels of Port Glasgow in September 1896. At a Board of Trade enquiry it transpired that the master was unaware of alterations to the Scilly and Wolf Rock lights and, thinking he was close to Ushant, had accidentally steered his vessel onto the Western Rocks. The sole comment of the crew upon leaving the islands for the mainland was: 'Scilly is a wonderful place to be shipwrecked' — high tribute to the hospitality they had received. The ship's bell engraved with the name *Thornliebank*, was found by a diver in 1988 and taken to the mainland.

The rusting remains of the *Susanna* and the *Thornliebank* near Zantmans were very nearly joined by the 7,660 tons gross Red Star liner

Gothland, (ex-*Gothic*, ex-*Gothland*, ex-*Gothic*) at 4.30 pm on 23 June 1914, but fortunately the steamer was saved. Launched in 1893 by Harland & Wolff of Belfast, this four-masted, 490 ft-long vessel was on passage from Montreal to Rotterdam with a general cargo which included wheat and 500 tons of frozen meat. In addition to her 131 crew, she carried eighty-six passengers, of whom forty-eight were Belgian refugees deported from Montreal. After striking the Crim, it was possible to climb down into Nos 2 and 3 holds and see a glimmer of sand and rock through the holes in her bottom. Capt. Young of the Liverpool Salvage Association set about refloating her, and his first action was to build a false floor in No 3 hold, after which the level of water inside was reduced by compressed air and she floated clear. As she was pulled away from the rocks by tugs at 7.15 am on 27 June, her foremast fell out through the bottom. She was taken to St Mary's Roads and anchored near Nut Rock, after which she went on to Southampton under tow from the tugs *Linnet*, *Triton* and *Ranger* and lay at anchor off Netley for many months before being broken up.

A French three-masted wooden schooner, the *Leon Bonnat* of Bayonne, was the last wreck to occur on the Crim. Homeward bound from Cardiff for Bayonne with 600 tons of coal in February 1921, she started to leak during a gale in the Bristol Channel. Capt. Richard Chaigre sought shelter at Lundy but the gale swung round to the north and he was forced to run for Scilly. Round Island light was reached and there was every hope the ship would successfully round the Bishop and reach Mount's Bay, but a westerly gale set in, the tide took her inshore, and at noon on 2 February she struck the Crim, then floated clear again. The captain went below to investigate a peculiar tearing noise and saw her cargo literally falling out through an enormous hole in the ship's bottom, the inrush of water being only partially stemmed by the outgoing coal. Though the vessel sank within five minutes of striking, the crew were able to lower and man the lifeboat, but when, just before leaving his ship, the captain tried to throw a box containing his papers and valuables into the boat, it missed and fell into the sea. A week later it was washed ashore empty, near Tresco. Meanwhile, the Bishop keepers had seen the wreck occur and soon afterwards the lifeboat *Elsie* arrived on the scene and took the twelve men aboard.

The Gunners, already mentioned in connection with the *Ardencraig*, claimed HMS *Hind*, an eight-gun ketch on 11 December 1668, and is also said to have been struck by the Dutch East Indiaman *Hollandia* in July 1743, before she went on to sink near St Agnes, an incident mentioned in Chapter three. A Maryport brig named *Bassenthwaite*, a four-year-old uninsured vessel, struck a partially submerged wreck at the entrance to Broad Sound on 7 April 1836 during a full north-west gale and sank immediately. She was on passage from Liverpool to Quebec with a general cargo, and though ten of her crew were able to escape in the ship's boats, the cook and the cabin boy were both lost in the wreck. A schooner from Surinam to London, the *Challenger*, Jones master, struck either the Nundeeps or the Gunners and was wrecked on 21 November 1843. Her crew landed on Bryher, as a result of which the complete island was put in quarantine. At various times since, several small vessels have met with a similar fate, for the Gunners lie dangerously close to the entrance to Broad Sound.

Understandably, in an area with so many hazards as the Western Rocks, there have been innumerable wrecks about which little or nothing is known. A ship, the *Providentia Devina* of Venice, Pascal Malena master, laden with soap, oil and brandy from Marseilles to Ostend, went down on 13 August 1782 with the loss of two lives, the rest of the crew escaping in a boat. Oranges floating around the rocks in large numbers on 21 February 1812 were the sure signs of a wreck, thought to be Spanish, but her identity remains unknown since she was lost with all hands. The *York*, Capt. Farthing, Seville to London, was lost on 5 February 1822, and the South Shields barque

"Gothland".

Janus on 27 December 1824, which with the assistance of a great number of local boats of all sizes was got safely alongside the quay at St Mary's. Other losses included an unidentified ship known to have been registered in Newfoundland, from which only three bodies were recovered in the November of 1829. A Scarborough-owned brig, the *George Lockwood* of 290 tons, laden with timber from Quebec for London, got amongst the Western Rocks on 19 December 1837 but managed to reach Penzance safely, where she was beached in a waterlogged condition. The *William Preston*, a South Shields vessel, was lost on 12 February 1842 near Melledgan whilst on her maiden voyage from Odessa with wheat. Two water-casks bearing the ship's name, found ashore on St Agnes, were the first clues to her loss.

After the Red Star liner *Gothland* struck and remained fast on the Crim Rocks on 23 June 1914, it was said it was possible to see the glimmer of sand through holes in her hull. When she was pulled clear on the 27th her foremast fell out through the bottom!

Today, these are nothing more than names with little meaning to anyone, yet, at the time, many were major disasters to those concerned. leaving families bereaved of father or sons, and if, as was often the case, the master was sole or part owner, bringing financial ruin as well. And the list of ships which have struck on the Western Rocks is almost endless; a brig, the *Ceredig* on 22 September 1865, which was eventually saved; the Norwegian barque *Kong Svere* with coal on 21 August 1896, and many others. Truly, these dangerous rocks have claimed more than their fair share of victims.

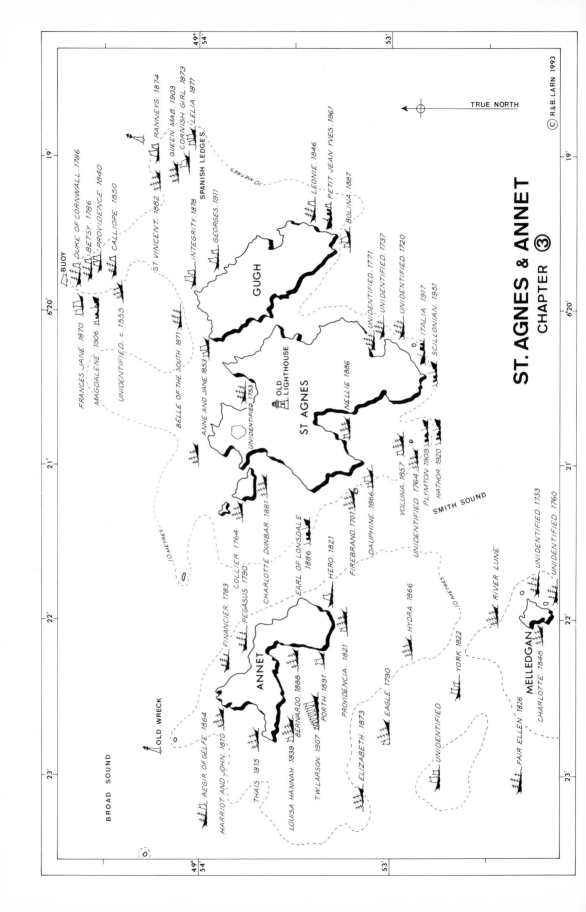

ST. AGNES & ANNET
CHAPTER ③

TRUE NORTH

© R.&B. LARN 1993

BROAD SOUND

OLD WRECK

ANNET

GUGH

ST AGNES

OLD LIGHTHOUSE

SMITH SOUND

MELLEDGAN

BUOY

SPANISH LEDGES

10 METRES

10 METRES

10 METRES

RANNEYS. 1874
QUEEN MAB. 1903
CORNISH GIRL. 1873
LELIA. 1871
ST VINCENT. 1882
INTEGRITY. 1878
GEORGES. 1911
LEONIE. 1846
PETIT JEAN YVES. 1961
BOLINA. 1887
DUKE OF CORNWALL. 1786
BETSY. 1786
PROVIDENCE. 1840
CALLIOPE. 1850
FRANCES JANE. 1870
MAGDALENE. 1906
UNIDENTIFIED. c. 1555
BELLE OF THE SOUTH. 1871
ANNE AND JANE. 1853
UNIDENTIFIED. 1753
UNIDENTIFIED. 1771
UNIDENTIFIED. 1737
UNIDENTIFIED. 1720
ITALIA. 1917
SCILLONIAN. 1951
NELLIE. 1886
VOLUNA. 1857
PLYMTON. 1909
HATHOR. 1920
UNIDENTIFIED. 1764
FINANCIER. 1783
COLLIER. 1764
PEGASUS. 1790
CHARLOTTE DUNBAR. 1881
EARL OF LONSDALE. 1886
HERO. 1821
FIREBRAND. 1707
DAUPHINE. 1866
AEGIR OF GELFE. 1864
HARRIOT AND JOHN. 1810
THAIS. 1815
LOUISA HANNAH. 1839
BERNARDO. 1888
T.W. LARSON. 1907
PORTH. 1891
PROVIDENCIA. 1821
ELIZABETH. 1873
EAGLE. 1790
HYDRA. 1866
UNIDENTIFIED
YORK. 1822
RIVER LUNE
FAIR ELLEN. 1826
CHARLOTTE. 1848
UNIDENTIFIED. 1733
UNIDENTIFIED. 1760

3

St Agnes and Annet Islands

'Good night father, good night mother, Good night friends and foes, God send a ship ashore before morning.'

DUE to their physical and intimate connection with the Western Rocks, St Agnes and neighbouring Annet were once the centre of wreck activity at Scilly. The pilot-gigs and lifeboat of St Agnes were usually the first to reach any wreck in the area, and there was once a time when few mornings passed in succession before the 'wrecker's prayer' was answered and some unfortunate vessel was found ashore. Children learnt the prayer from an early age, for a good wreck would support the entire community throughout a winter, always a time of shortages and desperate want amongst the islanders of those days. And such prayers, inhuman though they may seem to us today, were by no means peculiar to the island of Scilly. On lonely Tristan da Cunha, for example, infinitely more isolated than Scilly, the young maidens were taught: 'Please God send us a good shipwreck so we can get married.'[1]

St Agnes's association with shipwrecks goes back a very long way, well before the reign of Richard I (1189-99), when the island was named Hagness, or Hagenes. According to legend, which so often has an element of truth, it was here that St Warna landed, having reached Scilly from Ireland in a coracle. St Warna is said to have been the islanders' patron saint of shipwrecks, and if this is true he could not have landed at a more appropriate spot. A cove on the southern side of the island still bears the saint's name, and there yet survives the remains of a wishing-well into which the islanders once dropped pins, or coins when they could afford the luxury. If wrecks were asked for in return for their offerings, then the occupants of St Agnes could have been in little doubt as to their saint's ability. Even the island church came about as a result of a wreck, built

from the proceeds of a French vessel lost near Gorregan, the bell of which still calls the faithful to prayer.

Offshore from the two islands can be found many reefs and rocks which reach up to the surface from deep water, some with names associated with wrecks now long forgotten. Northwest of Annet lies an outcrop called Old Wreck, whilst off St Agnes can be found the Bristolman, Barrel of Butter, Spanish Ledges, Beady Pool and Boy's Rock, all of which have been the setting for some maritime disaster. The latter two are both associated with the same wreck, though their names are not to be found on any chart or ordnance survey map since Beady Pool is really Wingletang Bay and Boy's Rock only an outcrop in the shallows. Long ago a large Venetian ship, carrying a general cargo which included glass beads for the natives of Africa, went ashore here and was lost with all hands. The body of a young boy, a member of her luckless crew, was found wedged against this particular rock, hence its local name. To this day, a few minutes' patient digging in the sandbanks above high-water mark will uncover some of the dark-brown, red and clear beads which were once part of this cargo. Over the years, sufficient have been recovered for the St Mary's museum to string and put on display.

From afar, the most prominent feature of St Agnes is the old lighthouse, now disused after two and a half centuries of continuous service. A squat, circular structure painted white, it showed a warning light to mariners from October 1680 until September 1911, when it was rendered obsolete by the Peninnis beacon on neighbouring St Mary's. The first proposal for a light at Scilly is thought to have been submitted in 1665 by Sir John Coryton of Newton Ferrers, but to have been denied him following strong opposition by the Trinity Brethren. This application by Sir John was

The RMSS *Scillonian* missed the entrance to St Mary's Sound in fog on 10 September 1951, and drove ashore on Wingletang Ledge, St Agnes, but fortunately floated clear at high water with only a damaged rudder.

refuted by the Lighthouse Commissioners in 1861, who insisted that the first was a three-fold application submitted in 1679 by a Sir John Clayton, the East India Company, and prominent merchants of the Port of London. Whatever the truth of the matter, Trinity House obtained the first patent, the three-storied building was erected, and exhibited its first light on 30 October 1680. The light came from an open coal fire, burnt in a huge iron grate, or 'cresset', over a brick platform, to which was attached a pair of leather bellows to create the necessary draught. When burning well the light was visible from Land's End, but there were many occasions when the fire was barely discernible from St Mary's, or went out completely, either by design or neglect on the part of the keepers. In later years, the coal fire

was replaced by oil burning Argand lamps, and the massive 'cresset' found its way to Tresco, where it can still be seen in the abbey grounds.

The earliest wreck authenticated on St Agnes was that of a Dutch vessel, lost on Great Wingletang Rock in 1720, along with her entire crew and cargo, after which it was not until 1917 that the Wingletang claimed a vessel of any note. This was the steamer *Italia* of Spezia, which went ashore the same dark, foggy night that sent another steamer, the *Lady Charlotte*, crashing on to the rocks at Porth Hellick, St Mary's, less than four miles to the east. Although the *Italia* went down under the Italian flag, she had for the greater part of her career flown the red ensign as the *Gulf of Florida*. Built for the Greenock Steamship Co by Hawthorn Leslie & Co of Newcastle in 1891, this 2,792 tons gross vessel joined a fleet of seven Gulf ships which included the *Gulf of Ancud* and the *Gulf of Panama*. Rigged as a two-masted schooner, she was designed to carry six passengers and sixty-three crew, a phenomenal number for a relatively small ship. In 1910 she was bought out of British service by the Dall Orso Co of Genoa, who changed her name and port of registry. As the *Italia*, C. Aicaroi master, she left Cardiff for Taranto with coal on 9 May 1917. Whilst groping around the Scillies on 11 May in dense fog, she went aground at 3.30 pm in such a position that her stern almost touched the Great Wingletang Rock, her bows to the south-west. Shortly before striking, there had been some confusion on the bridge as to the ship's position, brought about by hearing voices and the sound of escaping steam around Newfoundland Point where the *Lady Charlotte* had already met with disaster and become a total loss. There was only one witness to the sinking of the *Italia*, a young girl on St Agnes who saw the dim outline of the wreck during a break in the fog. By the time the weather had cleared, the steamer had gone down and no one believed her story. Wreckage seen was presumed to have come from the *Lady Charlotte* and when finally the *Italia's* crew, none of whom spoke English, reached St Mary's, it was assumed that their ship had been torpedoed offshore. Thereafter, the wreck lay undisturbed and unsalvaged until 1964, when it was located and purchased by the author. Positive identification came from the slender shred of evidence offered by the serial number of the ship's patent log, an instrument which records the distance a ship has travelled through the water.

Had the sea been anything but flat calm on 10 September 1951, the Wingletang Ledges would certainly have claimed the islands' packet steamer *Scillonian*. Feeling her way across from Penzance on a day excursion trip in thick fog, the packet missed the entrance to St Mary's Sound and went aground. Her fifty-four passengers were taken on to Hugh Town by the company launch *Kittern*, which also went ashore, this time on Rat Island, at the entrance to Hugh Town harbour. Fortunately, they managed to get off again with nothing worse than a badly damaged rudder, whilst the *Scillonian* floated clear at high water, none the worse for the incident, her second stranding in

nine years. East from Wingletang, the sea shallows as it swings round into Wingletang Bay and on towards the sandbar linking St Agnes with the island of Gugh. Apart from the early Venetian wreck already mentioned, the only other incident here was that of an unidentified vessel which stranded and sank during a south-east gale in 1737, with the loss of her master and one seaman.

On Gugh itself, another unidentified ship was lost with all hands in 1771, probably on Cuckolds Ledge; the brig *Leonie* went onto the Bow on 4 January 1846; a Caernarvon schooner struck south of the island in 1887 and a French trawler, the *Petit Jean Yves*, went ashore in 1961. The *Leonie,* laden with brandy for Liverpool and the Clyde, missed stays when entering and struck so heavily that her masts had to be cut down in order to get her off. The Caernarvon schooner was the *Bolina*, carrying slates from Port Madoc to London, and she became a total wreck on 12 January 1887 during an easterly gale. The trawler *Petit Jean Yves* went aground near Cuckolds Carn on 9 March. The St Mary's lifeboat rescued her crew of five at night, returned them on board the next day and completed the service by successfully refloating the trawler on the next high water.

Less than half a mile offshore from Gugh, to the east, lie the Spanish Ledges, marked with a bell-buoy since 1873 to ensure that ships pass them on the correct side. The proposal made by Benjamin Tucker in 1810 to make a large anchorage at Scilly would have linked Dropnose on Gugh with Round rock and Spanish Ledges by a huge breakwater, but nothing ever came of the idea. It is assumed that the reef derived its name from some early wreck connection, but surprisingly enough in view of its exposed position there are few recorded incidents here and only one total loss. On 13 October 1871, the French schooner *Lelia*, Neath to Rochelle with coal, went onto the ledges but managed to get clear, whereas the Mousehole sailing-lugger *Cornish Girl* struck on Round rock in fine, clear weather on 10 June 1873 and sank so quickly that her crew barely had time to launch a boat. The Fowey-owned schooner *Ranneys*, with coal from Cardiff for Palermo, also struck the Spanish Ledges on 10 March 1874 and was saved, as was the *Queen Mab*, the largest of all these vessels, on 20 September 1903.

The *Queen Mab* was a steel barque of 1,027 tons gross and the valiant efforts made to save her rank high among the many outstanding feats of salvage performed at Scilly. One hundred and five days out from Punta Arenas, Chile, with fustic log-wood, this Glasgow-registered barque passed the Wolf Rock light-house during the early hours of 18 September 1903, tacking southward into the teeth of a

strong south-easterly. By dawn the following day, the anticipated time of her arrival at Falmouth, the crew were still having to wear ship at every watch and she was some twenty-four miles from her destination. By midnight that same day, the wind freshened to a full easterly gale and, having made no further progress towards Falmouth, Capt. Boxhall was forced to turn back towards Scilly. As they neared the islands, a pilot jack was flown but when no gig came out in answer the captain decided to make for the roads unaided. Approaching the deep channel between St Agnes and St Mary's with only her topsails set, the vessel failed to weather the Spanish Ledges and passed inside of the buoy, her crew all unaware of the extent of the underwater damage she was sustaining as she bumped and ground over the shoal. As they cleared the reef, they were met by the St Agnes gig *O & M*, whose coxswain saved the vessel from almost certain destruction on

After striking Spanish Ledges and only narrowly avoiding Bartholemew Ledges as she entered St Mary's Sound, the barque *Queen Mab* anchored off Samson on 20 September 1903 but was fast taking in water. She just made the shallows of Hugh Town harbour, watched by a great crowd.

Bartholomew Ledges, another set of rocks just ahead of the Spanish Ledges. Capt. Boxhall was advised to anchor his ship off the Tail of Samson in nine fathoms, and only then was it noticed that the barque was settling fast with the sea pouring into her hold. By 8 am the water level inside the vessel had reached 8 ft, and she was abandoned by all except her master and pilot Hicks. Shortly afterwards, the St Mary's lifeboat arrived alongside, whereupon the barque's crew reboarded and, assisted by the thirteen local men, began pumping. The St Agnes lifeboat, *James and Caroline*, also came out, having been launched with great difficulty by islanders wading waist deep in Periglis. Her crew also boarded the *Queen Mab* and with their assistance a second pump was got going. To encourage the men, Capt. Boxhall offered them £2.10s per head if his vessel sank, but £56 if she could be kept afloat until beached.

In the meantime, Mrs Boxhall and small son had been landed, along with some valuables and the ship's papers, and a request had been made for the assistance of the island packet-steamer *Lyonnesse*. Unfortunately, she was then aground in the harbour at low water, but as soon as the tide served the packet left Hugh Town and by 1.30 pm had reached the distressed barque, now with 13 ft of water in her hold. By then, the men aboard had been pumping continuously for five hours and were almost exhausted, but still managed to keep the pumps going while Capt. Tiddy of the *Lyonnesse* took the barque in tow and brought her towards Hugh Town harbour where she was again in trouble, drifting amongst some French boats and finally going aground at the harbour entrance. Men were put to work on her day and night, patching two holes in the port bow and repairing the underwater damage, while others recovered the anchors and cable she had slipped when taken in tow. Mr Banfield, the Lloyd's agent, inspected the vessel after she had been pumped dry and valued her hull at £4,500, her cargo at £2,729 and additional freight and materials at £1,070. All concerned were well rewarded for their services, and a notable feat of salvage was happily ended on 7 October when the Falmouth tug *Triton* towed the *Queen Mab* away to Falmouth and then on to Le Havre.

Another incident involving the Spanish Ledges occurred on 24 April 1882, when the barque *St Vincent* of London struck heavily on the westward side of the reef but bore away for Crow Sound, only to sink at anchor off Tolls Island, near Pelistry, and this despite the fact that a St Agnes pilot, Israel Hicks, was aboard. En route from the West Indies and St Vincent for London with sugar, the 479 tons gross *St Vincent* had been built in 1867 by Clarke of Jersey, for T. Sorulton of London.

Mid-way between Gugh and St Mary's lie the Bartholomew Ledges, a rock outcrop with 40 ft of water on three sides, and dangerously sited in the centre of an otherwise unobstructed fairway. The names of at least seven vessels which struck the ledges are recorded, but there must have been dozens of others whose names are forgotten. Amongst the many fragments of wreck scattered underwater on and around the Ledges, are the remains of what is possibly the oldest known shipwreck in the Isles of Scilly. Discovered in 1978 by Michael Pirie, some 60 boat-shaped lead ingots weighing around 80lbs each were recovered, along with five tons of bronze bell fragments and other artefacts, before the site was designated by the Secretary of State as being of historic importance. The remains are now believed to be that of a small armed Spanish or Spanish/Netherlands cargo vessel, the evidence coming from six breech loading cannon, a number of silver two reale coins of the reigns of Ferdinand and Isabella (1474-1504), Ferdinand and Johanna (1504-1506) and Charles V (1521-1555), and other artefacts. On Christmas Eve 1786, two vessels were lost, the Penzance brigantine *Duke of Cornwall* and the Chester brig *Betsy*. The former was the Duke of Cornwall's private tin ship, carrying a general cargo from London to Falmouth, Thomas Hoskin master. She had to be run ashore on St Agnes, where 'very little of her cargo was saved for the proprietors'. The *Betsy*, Williams master, Chester to London

Above: The Boulogne steam-trawler *Magdeleine*, wrecked on Bartholemew Ledge, 3 June 1906, when she passed the ledge buoy on the wrong side by mistake.

Previous page: Local pilot gigs and cutters removing ships stores, cargo and valuables from the wreck of the Newcastle registered *Earl of Lonsdale*, following her wreck off Troy Town, St Agnes, 8 June 1885.

with lead blocks and empty casks, struck and carried on for a short distance, finally sinking between Bartholomew and Perconger. *Providence*, Hoare master, a 99 ton Dartmouth schooner, hit the ledges on 29 December 1840 and had to be run ashore on St Agnes but was saved, whilst the Greek brig *Calliope*, Consalapulo master, Odessa to Falmouth, had to be put on the Garrison shore near Woolpack Battery, St Mary's, in order to save the vessel on 30 October 1850. With her cargo ruined and hull badly damaged, the *Calliope* was sold for £22.10s. An Irish schooner of Carrickfergus, the *Frances Jane*, Runcorn to Plymouth with salt, was another victim on 28 May 1870, but got off. Only the seventh and last victim left her ribs and plating to rust on the bottom around Bartholomew Ledges, this being the Boulogne steam-trawler *Magdaleine*. She

entered St Mary's Roads in search of medical assistance for an injured seaman on 2 June 1906, and unwittingly passed the wrong side of the ledges buoy. Fortunately, the tide being full, she cleared the rocks and reached the anchorage safely The following day, on leaving for sea, her master again took her inside of the buoy, between Bartholomew and St Agnes, and this time she struck heavily at 7.35 pm and foundered two hours later.

Closer inshore to Gugh and St Agnes, a London barque, *Belle of the South*, Davis master, struck Perconger Ledges during a heavy rain squall on 7 July 1871. Fortunately for the owners, there was a pilot aboard at the time who got her off and she ran for St Mary's, making water fast. Beached near Hugh Town with 10 ft of water in her, she was pumped out and laid alongside the pier where a piece of Perconger rock, 2 ft long, was found embedded in her hull. On passage from London to Algoa Bay, the barque was carrying a general cargo. Other wreck incidents in the vicinity include the schooner *Anne & Jane* of Caernarvon, Pritchard master, which struck a rock north of St Agnes on 3 March 1853 while carrying slates from her home port to Perth. Local pilots assisted her to safety, a service for which they received £30. The *Integrity*, an Aberystwyth schooner of 98 tons net (sometimes quoted as the *Integrite*) was also aided by pilots who beached her in the vicinity of Perconger on 10 October 1878 after she had lost her foremast and longboat in heavy seas off the Bishop. Bound from Lisbon to Wicklow with lime phosphates, she became unmanageable in Smith Sound and drifted round the back of Annet before going ashore. Capt. E. Evans and three of the crew were saved, but a fourth man was swept overboard and drowned. She floated off on 12 October and was taken to St Mary's pier.

Whilst derelicts were not uncommon at sea, the crew of the St Mary's lifeboat, *Henry Dundas*, called out at 7.35 pm on 12 January 1911, were surprised to find the French ketch *Georges* of Auray at anchor in the roads near St Agnes, with a light burning but no one on board. Closer examination showed that the sea had flooded the cabin to floor level, and a smashed bulwark and broken rudder told their own story. The *Georges* had left Swansea on 10 January with 170 tons of coal for Trinite, but encountered a gale which carried away all her canvas and started a severe leak. After reaching St Mary's Sound in a sinking condition, her crew had abandoned her and landed safely on St Agnes, except for one man who broke a leg. Left at anchor overnight, the ketch slowly filled, and by morning had gone under. In 1753, a large unidentified vessel went ashore in Porth Killier, on the same day that the *Johanna*, Liverpool from the Isle of Wight, was wrecked

The Newcastle registered steamship *Earl of Lonsdale*, after she struck a shallow rock between the islands of Annet and St Agnes, 8 June 1885. The Troy Town maze in the foreground is of uncertain antiquity, said to date from pre history to a bored lighthouse keeper in 1729.

on Little Smith. Another ship with a similar name, the *Lady Johanna*, is also believed to have been wrecked on the same rock on 2 February 1782.

Burnt Island, which offered some protection to the old St Agnes lifeboat station from north-west winds which howled straight down the north channel, has been the site of two losses. A collier with fuel for the lighthouse was totally wrecked here in 1764, and on 18 January 1881 an 82-ton French brigantine was found ashore, and apparently abandoned. She was the 42-year-old wooden-hulled *Charlotte Dunbar* which had sailed from Newport for Audierne with coal, and run into a north-easter which had reached hurricane force. Nothing was ever heard of her master, Capt. Guillon, or his five-man crew.

It is difficult to imagine a more unlikely place for a steamer to be wrecked than the narrow channel separating St Agnes from Annet, but it was here that the steamer *Earl of Lonsdale*, Llewellin Davis master, was stranded at 3 am on 8 June 1885. Owned by Thomas G. Dunford of Newcastle, the vessel's port of registry, the *Earl of Lonsdale* was carrying beans and cotton seed from Alexandria to Portishead. While steaming recklessly at full-speed in dense fog, the lookout on her forecastle sighted breakers ahead but no sooner had course been altered to clear them than she struck a submerged rock and remained fast, water pouring into the engine-room. Shortly after, the fog lifted and no one was more surprised than the captain to see the Troy Town maze and St Agnes lighthouse close abeam. He had thought his ship to have been west and at least ten miles south of the Bishop when she struck, whereas in fact she had entered the Western Rocks and got into Smith Sound, heading straight for St Agnes. It was remarkable that she had penetrated so deep without striking earlier. With her hull pierced in several places, salvage was out of the question, and the 1,543 tons gross vessel, which had been built at North Shields in 1872, had to be abandoned as a total loss. Four days later the wreck was sold by Mr J. Hooper for £67 to a London purchaser, whilst 900 tons of her bean cargo went to a Mr W. Rogers for twenty-two shillings, who in turn sold them to local farmers. Within the month the wreck itself changed hands, being bought by Vasey and Co of Newcastle, who were able to remove such of the machinery as was worth salvage before the vessel broke in two on 27 August. South of St Agnes. on the verge of Smith Sound, lie the Lethegus and Shooting Rocks which guard the entrance to St Warnas Cove. This area is littered with the wreckage of ships, including possibly that of three large French men o'war and two relatively modern steamers.

The tactical value of Scilly as a base in enemy hands has fortunately never been put to the test, although Cornishmen once repeatedly petitioned successive governments to increase the size of the garrison in order to better defend the islands. Scilly has not, in fact, been invaded since the days of the Vikings, but may have close to it on 10 October 1781 when it would appear that the French sent a small fleet of troop laden men o'war to capture the islands. The incident is shrouded in mystery, and would benefit from some in-depth research amongst French naval archives. If the known details are true, then in fact the Scillies witnessed a second naval disaster, equal in terms of lives lost, if not worse, to that of Sir Clowdisley Shovell in 1707. Despite there being no tangible evidence of the event, a legend persists in Scillonian history that a French warship sank a few hundred metres from the westernmost point of St Agnes in 1800. Escorted by a frigate, the larger vessel, said to be of 74 guns sank, leaving only a 'tricoloured pennant attached to a mast or staff showing above the surface to mark the grave of over 600 men'. Bodies were said to have been buried in mass graves on St Agnes, and the ship identified as *L'Apollen*, but it is known she was lost off Land's End in May 1773, with all hands.

A Sherborne Mercury newspaper report in March 1781 states clearly that the *Conquerant*, third rate, 74 guns and 700 men; *Le Priarus*, third rate, 74 guns and 600 men, and the fifth rate *Julie*, a 44 gun frigate with 340 men, were all wrecked off the Isles of Scilly, with the loss of all on board all three sips, a total of 1640 seamen. Leading up to this statement, are a number of intelligence reports and sightings of the French fleet in the Channel, and these three ships can be found frequently included in ship lists of the enemy, yet basic research into French records suggests two of the ship names did not exist at the time, and the *Conquerant* as still being in service after 1781. There is probably some hard fact in all this, and could be a worthwhile and rewarding research project.

A Padstow brig, the 336-ton *Voluna*, Bowden master, went ashore on the southern side of St Agnes during a dense fog on 1 June 1857 (the Board of Trade Wreck Register gives the date as 8 June) whilst in ballast from Falmouth for Quebec. Bo'sun Hodgson was on watch when she struck, and he and the rest of the crew managed to struggle ashore, leaving the *Voluna*, owned by Thomas Seaton of Padstow, to go to pieces in the surf. Another sailing ship to be lost here was the Danish brigantine *Nellie* of Elsinore, which struck first on Jackys Rock, out amongst the Western Rocks on 26 March 1886. Part of the vessel drifted onto Annet, the remainder into St Warnas cove. Launched at St Johns, New Brunswick, in 1866 as the *Julia Lingley*, this 316-ton wooden vessel had been in collision west of Scilly and had driven helpless before a full south-westerly gale onto the Western Rocks. The second mate and four seamen, who managed to reach Melledgan after three hours on a raft, were forced to quench their thirst with puffins' blood until rescued by a local gig. Later, one seaman and the ship's carpenter were saved after having clung to part of the wreck for sixteen hours. Commanded by Capt. M. L. Svendsen, who lost his life in the wreck along with his chief officer, the *Nellie* was on passage from Bordeaux to Cardiff with pit props.

Lethegus rocks, which claimed a wine-laden Dutch galliot in 1764, is better known for its steamship wrecks, the first of which occurred in 1909. This led to the remarkable coincidence referred to in Chapter 1, when two steamers lay on the seabed, piled one upon the other like

The forward section of the steamship *Plympton* following her partial capsize during the afternoon of 22 July 1906 on Lethegus Rocks. Two local boatmen and a visitor engaged in 'wrecking' at the time she turned over, were sucked down and only the visitor escaped alive.

broken toys in a nightmare of twisted steel. The *Plympton* of London, a Commercial Steamship Co vessel, was the first of the pair to sink, after going ashore in thick fog on 14 August while carrying maize in bags from Villa Constitution to Dublin, via Falmouth. Her arrival was not exactly unannounced, since she steamed headlong onto the rocks with her fog siren going full blast. An old gig, the *Dolly Varden*, was launched from Porthcressa and after searching around Gugh and the Wingletang area, found the *Plympton* with her bows hard and fast ashore, listing heavily to port. After her crew of twenty-three had been landed, the islanders set about the age-old practice of stripping the wreck. That afternoon, whilst work was still in progress, the flood tide gently lifted the steamer off the rocks, and without warning she fell on her port side and sank, leaving only the bow section above water. Two local men, Charles Mumford of St Mary's and Charles Hicks of St Agnes, were sucked down by the wreck and drowned, several others having lucky escapes; one in particular, a visitor to Scilly named Ormrod, was actually inside the deckhouse when the steamer capsized. He went down with her but managed to escape through a porthole and reached the surface still clutching his trophy, the saloon steward's dinner bell! It was said at the time that his hair turned completely white as a result of the experience. Built for Furness, Withy & Co of West Hartlepool in 1893, the *Plympton*, 314 ft in length and of 2,869 tons gross was declared a total loss, her value for insurance purposes being set at £16,000, with her cargo at an additional £25,000. A local newspaper report of the incident stated that 'the position is bad and it is doubtful if any further salvage will be possible. Her after part lies in 15 fathoms, her bows sticking up almost perpendicular and very dangerous'.[2]

The final act in this drama occurred on 2 December 1920, when the big German steamer *Hathor*, of 7,060 tons gross, sank right across the wreck of the *Plympton* at the base of the Lethegus Rocks. Built by J. C. Tecklenborg A. G., Geestemunde, in 1912, the *Hathor* of

Hamburg had been interned in a Chilean port for the duration of World War I, during which time her machinery suffered badly from neglect. After the war she was released, loaded with nitrate of soda and oil cake at Arica, and sailed for Portland but broke down near the Azores. Whilst under tow from two German tugs, she was abandoned in a gale off Scilly after the towing hawsers had parted. The St Mary's lifeboat *Elsie* went out in response to a distress call and found the steamer with both anchors down, dragging towards the shore, and only her five officers on board, the other nineteen members of the crew having taken to the boats. After she had drifted onto the Lethegus, the officers were taken off in a difficult and dangerous rescue, one of them having a very lucky escape after falling between the ship's side and the lifeboat. He was saved from certain death by the prompt action of Bob Ellis, a member of the lifeboat crew, who thrust the first thing to hand into the fast narrowing gap. The improvised fender turned out to be a personal bundle belonging to the *Hathor's* captain, who thereby lost his clothes, papers, instruments and the ship's chronometer. Forty-six years later that same chronometer was found and brought to the surface by a diver, its gold-plated hands stopped for eternity at three minutes to eleven. The *Hathor* took her cargo to the bottom and little or no salvage was ever carried out on either of the two ships. Underwater the scene is indescribable, with a propeller and huge sections of ships rearing up from the seabed, boilers garlanded with anchor cable, shafting and connecting rods crossed with masts and derricks. The bow section of the *Plympton*, which in a photograph taken just before she sank clearly shows her bell hanging behind the windlass, now lies upside down and still intact, whilst the stern of the *Hathor* remains upright in 100 ft of water, a single kedge davit overhanging the rusting deck rail.

Due west from Priglis Bay across Smith Sound, lies Annet, uninhabited except for vast numbers of seabirds for whom the island is a sanctuary. Whilst St Agnes and Annet are very much a part of one another, it is the latter which offers the visitor the first real foretaste of the Western Rocks. The *Financier*, John Lobes master, Charlestown to London with rice, tobacco and indigo, was lost here on 5 September 1783; also the Admiralty sixth rate, 28 gun Pegasus of 594 tons, went ashore on Annet on 8 July 1790 but got off on the flood tide undamaged. Hellweathers, an aptly-named area and the scene of many small wrecks, claimed the 150-ton Spanish brig *Providencia*, a wool ship from St Andero for Bristol, on 2 October 1821 during a north-west gale accompanied by rain. The very next day, the Bryher-owned boat, the *Hero*, with twenty-one men aboard, was smashed to pieces by heavy seas whilst working cargo out of the Spaniard. Almost every able-bodied male and boat at Scilly was employed in recovering and landing the bales of wool, originally valued at £10 a ton but reduced to only £3 after their soaking in salt water.

Around dawn on 22 February 1839, in response to urgent signals from the St Agnes lighthouse, local boats went out amongst the Western Rocks and found a vessel wrecked on the Ranneys, half a mile west of Annet. Oranges and casks of wine lay thick on the surface, but only twenty-five casks and a small quantity of fruit were recovered before the tide turned and swept the remainder out to sea. Papers recovered from amongst the wreckage showed the ship to be the 165-ton brig *Louisa Hannah* of Poole, H. Moores master. Homeward bound from Lisbon, she was lost

The Valhalla figurehead collection open to the public on Tresco, now an 'out-station' of the National Maritime Museums responsibility, is a reminder of the many sailing ship wrecks around the Isles of Scilly.

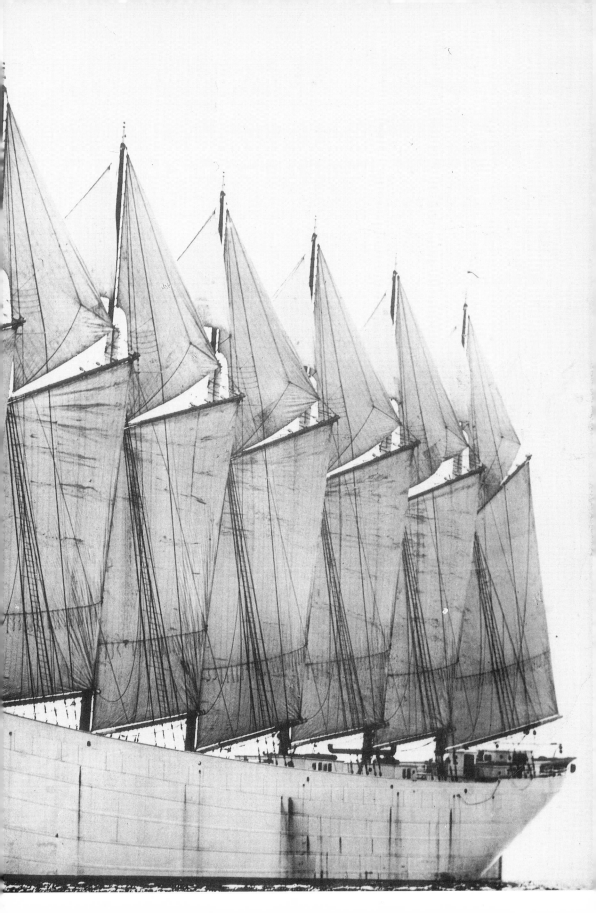

with all hands.

Muncoy Neck, the channel between Melledgan and Annet, is no place for a large vessel even in fine weather, let alone dense fog. On 27 July 1879, the 1,172 tons gross iron barque *River Lune* of Liverpool, in ballast from Lorient to Ardrossen in Scotland, was groping her way past the islands when the lookouts sighted rocks ahead and on both sides. George West, the master, ordered the helm hard down but she struck on Brothers Rock in coming round and began to sink. Her crew hastily abandoned ship when the stern went completely underwater, but reboarded later to collect personal belongings and some of the ship's fittings. At the subsequent Board of Trade enquiry, the master blamed his chronometer for any inaccuracy of navigation, his calculations and log-book entries showing his position as being at least ten or fifteen miles west of the Bishop light. Built at Wallsend in 1868, the *River Lune* was owned by John Hargrove of Chapel Street, Liverpool, and her wreck, when sold, fetched only £55. Her figurehead was recovered intact and can be seen in the Valhalla collection of ships' figureheads at Tresco.

Another barque, also in ballast, the *Bernardo* of Genoa, went ashore at the back of Annet on 11 March 1888. This 701-ton Italian vessel had lost all her sails during a west-north-west gale and, completely helpless, was blown ashore. Although one boat was successfully launched, it quickly capsized in the heavy seas, drowning its eleven occupants. Capt. Dapelo, who had remained on board, was forced to swim for his life when the vessel broke up beneath him, and managed to reach Old Woman Rock, to which he clung until rescued by fishermen. The 13-year-old *Bernardo*, owned by G. B. Degregori of Camogli, Italy, quickly went to pieces in the surf and nothing of value was saved. The 34-ton smack *Porth* of Padstow, John Billing master, although much smaller, was another

wreck in the same area on 10 March 1891, the night of the 'Great Blizzard' that caused so much havoc in the West Country, the worst storm for 200 years. With a crew of three, she had sailed from Swansea on 2 March with sixty tons of culm destined for St Colomb Minor. After wasting six days sheltering in Mumbles, she sailed at 4 pm on the 8th, but during the following night, both gangways, the cookhouse and water-closet were washed away in the gale, her boat was stove in and the ship's bulwarks damaged. Whilst entering St Mary's Roads via Broad Sound, she ran ashore on the Minmanueth Rocks. The ten-oared St Agnes lifeboat *James & Caroline* rescued the master and his son, but the third member of the crew, Charles Boxer, was found frozen to death high above the tide line.

In 1907 there occurred a wreck which has become almost legend amongst seafarers and certainly amongst the islanders of Scilly. This was the gigantic steel schooner *Thomas W. Lawson*, one of the largest pure sailing vessels the world has known, and certainly the largest vessel to be wrecked here until comparatively recent years. The *Lawson*, to use the name by which she became known locally, began her relatively short career on the slipway of the Fore River Engineering Co of Quincy, Massachusetts in 1902. Built at a time when sail was battling with steam for survival, she was an attempt to prove that huge sailing vessels with small crews were both practical and more economical, in comparison to their dirty, smoke-belching rivals. Her tonnage and other statistics were impressive, to say the least. She was 395 ft in length and carried twenty-five sails totalling 40,612 sq ft of canvas on seven masts when under full spread. Her tonnage – 5,218 tons gross, 4,914 net and 5,006 under deck – combined to give her a deadweight cargo capacity of 7,500 tons and an overall displacement of over 10,000 tons, the vessel being entirely wind-driven. Any steamer of comparable size would have carried a crew numbering between thirty-five to fifty, whilst a conventional full-rigged ship would certainly have had twenty-eight, yet the *Lawson* managed

Previous page: Built in an attempt to show that very large schooners could be operated more economically than steamships, the *Thomas W. Lawson*, built in 1902, required only eighteen crew.

with only eighteen! Designed to be worked by a minimum crew, there were many mechanical aids on deck, including donkey engines at the foot of each mast. This made it unnecessary for men to go aloft to work sail, and greatly facilitated the handling of sheets and braces.

Her last voyage began on 20 November 1907 when, under the command of Capt. Geoffrey Dow, the huge vessel left Philadelphia for London with almost two and a quarter million gallons of paraffin oil in drums, valued at £40,000. In crossing the Atlantic, two bad gales in succession were encountered, so that upon sighting Scilly not a single boat remained intact on its chocks, and she had only six serviceable sails left. On Friday, 13 December 1907, a traditionally unlucky day, the *Lawson* reached the Bishop but, because of a tidal set, found herself well inside of the lighthouse and virtually trapped within the Western Rocks. The schooner was brought to anchor in Broad Sound, where it was anticipated she would ride out the rough seas brought on by a north-west gale. Ashore, her plight had not gone unnoticed, since the St Agnes lifeboat was launched and reached the sailing vessel at 5 pm. To the surprise of the lifeboat's coxswain, Capt. Dow refused his offer of assistance and only reluctantly accepted the services of William Cook Hicks, known locally as Billy Cook, a Trinity House pilot. The St Mary's lifeboat also put out, but broke her mast under the counter of the *Lawson* when going alongside and had to return, taking with her orders to telegraph Falmouth for tugs. As the wind freshened from the north, so the seas increased, and soon the St Agnes lifeboat was forced to leave, not only on account of the weather conditions but also because one of the crew had collapsed and was in urgent need of medical attention. As they pulled clear of the pitching schooner, the final instructions given to Billy Cook were for him to burn a flare if the situation deteriorated further and the services of the lifeboat were again needed.

Between 2.30 and 2.50 am on Saturday, 14 December, it was noticed that the schooner's lights had vanished, but since no flare had been sighted, it was assumed that all was still well on board. In fact, the *Thomas W. Lawson* had already become a total loss but no one ashore could have known, and in the complete darkness the watchers on St Agnes could only maintain their anxious vigil. Daybreak revealed a mass of floating wreckage around St Agnes and Annet, and the fate of the world's largest schooner became apparent. Regardless of personal danger in the appallingly high seas which were then running, a volunteer crew speedily launched the six-oared gig *Slippen* to search the outlying rocks and islands for survivors. Manned by eight men from St Agnes, five of whom were named Hicks, the gig put out and soon human forms could be seen on Annet, but the seas were then far too rough for a landing to be made. Later when a landing was achieved, only corpses were found at first, but a further search found a seaman, George Allen of Battersea, injured but alive and he was quickly taken back to St Agnes. That afternoon the *Slippen*, still manned by the same crew, put to sea again, rowing as far as Hellweathers where two more survivors were sighted. These proved to be Capt. Dow and the *Lawson's* engineer, Edward Rowe of Boston, both of whom were saved after an heroic rescue by Frederick Cook Hicks, the eldest son of the pilot who had lost his life in the wreck. Freddie Cook swam a line to the injured men through raging surf, bringing them back one at a time. Mr Jack Hicks, the last survivor of the crew that manned the *Slippen* that day until his recent death, was presented with a gold watch by the United States government, for his service in the St Agnes lifeboat. Each member of the gig's crew received a gold medal, and it is fitting that the old *Slippen* herself has not been forgotten. Refitted, the gig has found a permanent home on the mainland at Newquay, where it is held in trust.

The full story of the wreck was pieced together from the two survivors. After the St Agnes lifeboat had left the moored vessel, the gale increased until it reached 90 mph. At about 1.15 am, first the port cable parted, then the starboard, and the *Lawson* was adrift and being blown towards Annet. Capt. Dow, the engineer, the mate, a steward and pilot Hicks all took to the mizzen rigging. Less than fifteen minutes later the vessel struck west of Carn Irish, dealing her starboard side a mighty blow. She then broke in two between Nos 4 and 5 holds and collapsed on her side on Shag Rock, throwing all on board into the sea. Until recently it has always been accepted that the wreck occurred on the outside of Minmanueth, to the west of the Haycocks, but this was not the case. The wreck of the *Thomas W. Lawson* was successfully relocated in 1969, when it was found that the two sections are almost a quarter of a mile apart, the bow section to the north-

east of Shag Rock, the stern to the south-west, both in 50 ft of water.

Melledgan, a small uninhabited island one mile south of Annet, has claimed three ships. One was a ship whose name is now forgotten which was carrying mahogany from the Bay of Honduras to London and went ashore here in 1733, only her captain and one seaman escaping. They drifted around on a raft for two days before getting ashore on Kitten Rock, north of Gugh, where they were found days later. The second was a Dutchman, loaded with wine and paper, which was lost on the Biggal of Melledgan in 1760, while the third, the 350-ton Swedish brig *Charlotte*, foundered on Christmas Day 1848. Loaded with deals and balk timber from Gothenburg for Montevideo, the *Charlotte's* master, mate, two seamen and a passenger lost their lives in the wreck. The ten survivors erected a rough tent

Dense fog caused the RMS. *Scillonian* to goashore on Newford Island 1942, where she lay for a whole tide, until refloated. Although armed with a small AA. gun behind her funnel, the *Scillonian* was never once attacked during WW.2

on the rock, where they spent a bleak and cheerless night before being sighted and rescued by a passing boat.

Whilst the wreck locations of the fifty or so ships already mentioned are reasonably well documented, as in other parts of Scilly or Cornwall for that matter, there have been many incidents with only a vague geographical location. Reports in local newspapers or records of such incidents merely state 'lost off St Agnes', or, 'ashore amongst the Western Rocks', but if this is to be a faithful record they must also receive a mention. One such vessel was the brigantine *Eagle* of Charlestown, John Rosseter master, laden with tobacco, rice and staves, ashore near St Agnes on 5 June 1790; others were the *Harriet & John*, sloop of 69 tons, N. Baker, master and owner, ashore in November 1810, and the *Thais* of Penzance, 29 October 1815, both of which were saved. A schooner, the *York* of Chichester, James Farthing master, carrying a cargo of oranges from Seville to London, was lost with all hands on 4 February 1822; the *Fair Ellen* went ashore, but was saved later on 7 September 1826, and two local pilot boats were wrecked in the same area early in January 1831. An unidentified schooner was lost on St Agnes on 2 April 1841; the Swedish brig *Aegir*, of Gelf, Malaga to St Petersburg with olive oil, struck on 1 May 1864, but was refloated later the same day, and the *Hydra*, a barque, was another victim on 6 February 1866. On the 13th of the same month, the French schooner *Dauphine* sailed from Scilly, but caught fire two hours later and became a total loss, her hulk eventually drifting onto St Agnes, not far from the spot where seven years later, on 15 March 1873, the *Elizabeth* was lost with all hands.

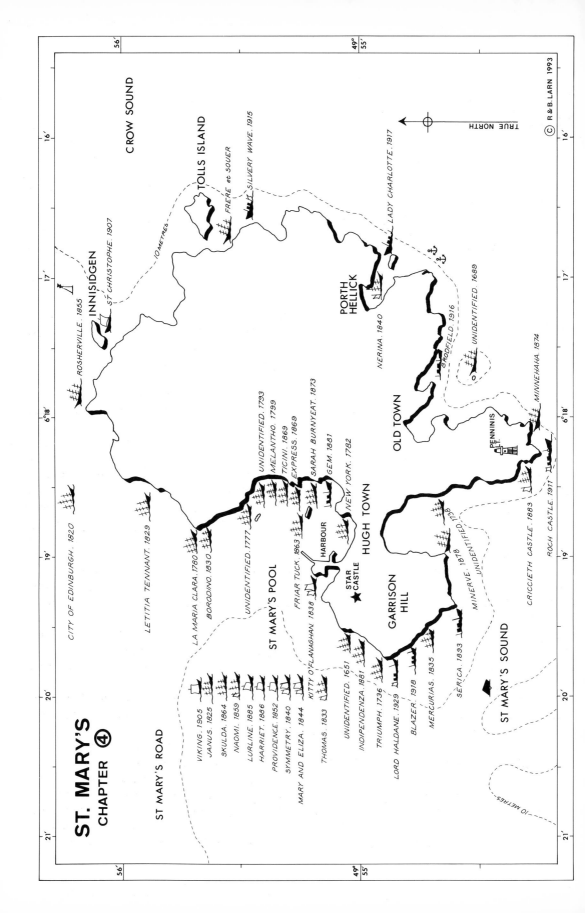

ST. MARY'S
CHAPTER ④

CROW SOUND

TOLLS ISLAND

INNISIDGEN

FRERE et SOUER

St. SILVERY WAVE. 1915

St CHRISTOPHE. 1907

ROSHERVILLE. 1855

10 METRES

PORTH HELLICK

LADY CHARLOTTE. 1917

⚓

NERINA. 1840

UNIDENTIFIED. 1689

BRODFIELD. 1916

OLD TOWN

CITY OF EDINBURGH. 1820

ST MARY'S ROAD

LETITIA TENNANT. 1829

LA MARIA CLARA. 1780

BORODINO. 1830

UNIDENTIFIED. 1777

UNIDENTIFIED. 1793

MELANTHO. 1799

TICINI. 1869

EXPRESS. 1869

SARAH BURNYEAT. 1873

GEM. 1881

NEW YORK. 1782

ST MARY'S POOL

FRIAR TUCK. 1863

KITTY O'FLANAGHAN. 1838

HARBOUR

HUGH TOWN

STAR CASTLE

GARRISON HILL

PENNINIS LT.

MINNEHAHA. 1874

MINERVE. 1878

UNIDENTIFIED. 1738

CRICCIETH CASTLE. 1883

ROCH CASTLE. 1911

VIKING. 1905

JANUS. 1825

SKULDA. 1864

NAOMI. 1859

LURLINE. 1885

HARRIET. 1886

PROVIDENCE. 1852

SYMMETRY. 1840

MARY AND ELIZA. 1844

THOMAS. 1833

UNIDENTIFIED. 1651

INDIPENDENZA. 1881

TRIUMPH. 1736

LORD HALDANE. 1929

BLAZER. 1918

MERCURIAS. 1835

SERICA. 1893

ST MARY'S SOUND

10 METRES

TRUE NORTH

© R & B. LARN 1993

4

St Mary's, the 'capital'

THE largest of all the islands, St Mary's became the centre or 'capital' of Scilly not solely on the merits of physical size but because it offered the best anchorages. It receives a measure of protection on three sides from other islands in the group, making St Mary's Pool and Porth Cressa into sheltered havens for shipping, with easy access to the open sea. A third anchorage, known as Old Town Bay, which is completely open to the south-east, was for centuries the chief landing-site and main settlement on the island, then known as Hencastle or Heyugcastle. A sod battery with cannon on Tolman Point, backed up by Ennor Castle overlooking the town, offered protection from a seaward attack, and it was to the latter fortification that Leyland referred when he commented, 'St Mary's, a five mile or more in cumpace, it is a poore town and a meately strong pile, but the rous of the buildings in it be sore defacid and woren'.[1] The gradual decline of the old town in favour of the newer Hugh Town was almost certainly brought about by the need for a larger and better protected anchorage, though legend says that it was the result of a curse placed upon Richard, Earl of Cornwall, for murdering a man of the church. Possibly monks residing at Holy Vale were said to levy a toll on all boats and persons landing, and controlled a chain boom from Tolman across the entrance. The Earl of Cornwall, upon hearing of this, disguised himself as a pilgrim and when refused permission to land unless he paid the fee, leapt over the barrier and struck the prior a mortal blow. Curse or not, Ennor certainly did fall into disuse. Two of the sod-battery guns were removed in 1767, the third in about 1820, and Old Town gradually dropped into the background of events.

There are, unfortunately, no reliable records of very early wrecks in this area, though dozens of small sailing vessels must have been lost on these headlands, or blown ashore. Troutbeck briefly dismisses them by saying 'Church Ledge Bay and Church Ledges, many vessels lost here, deep water all round'.[2] An unidentified transport vessel, outward bound, was lost on or near the Old Town Gilstone in 1689, having struck the Woolpack, south of the castle on Garrison Hill, and iron cannon and anchors have since been located on the seabed to support this story. One of these cannon was raised in 1964, but no identifying marks remained and it disintegrated shortly afterwards.

One of the better-known wrecks on St Mary's occurred at Peninnis, between the point and Pulpit Rock. This was the 845-ton wooden ship *Minnehaha* of Liverpool, Jones master, which had reached Falmouth on 16 January 1874 from Callao in Peru with a cargo of guano, and sailed for Dublin to discharge the following day. The weather deteriorated badly after she left, and soon a hard north-westerly gale was blowing. At 3 am on Sunday, 18 January, a light seen through the murk was assumed to be the Wolf Rock, and the captain ordered the helm to be put down. The Channel pilot, Capt. David Volk of Falmouth, shortly afterwards countermanded this order without the captain's knowledge, and within minutes the vessel had struck on the south-east corner of Peninnis, amongst the Jolly Rocks. She went ashore with all sail set, almost on top of the tide, and thumped the rocks so hard that a large hole was made in the port bow, into which the sea poured. (See picture, p 119) Within two minutes she was under water, and those who had not been swept away took to the rigging. Capt. Jones undressed in the mizzen-top and then, shouting 'With God's help I will save your lives',[3] sprang into the sea and was last seen swimming for the shore. Robert Thomas, the first mate, led the nine remaining survivors from the mizzen to the main shrouds, down the forestay and over the jib-boom onto the rocks. Shortly afterwards they met one of the islanders, Israel Pender, in Peninnis lane and told him of the wreck, St Mary's first knowledge of the tragedy which had occurred.

The pilot, Capt. Volk, who had survived a narrow escape in the Austrian brig *Slaven* under Pentire Cliffs at Padstow in March 1869, was drowned, along with the captain of the *Minnehaha* and several members of the crew. Had they followed the mate's example and waited in the rigging until daybreak, all would no doubt have been saved. Owned by Messrs Hughes of Menai, and built at St Johns, New Brunswick, in 1857, the *Minnehaha* had been fourteen months on passage from South America and was uninsured. Almost two months after her wreck, on Sunday, 15 March, Capt. Volk's body was recovered from the sea off St Eval cliffs, Padstow, and his funeral in Falmouth was attended by a large number of fellow Channel pilots and local officials. On 3 April that same year, the *Belle*, a Plymouth barge, dragged her anchors when a gale blew up while she was salvaging timbers from the wreck of the *Minnehaha*. She was driven ashore but managed to get off again later. The *Minnehaha's* bell has now found a permanent resting-place in the Isles of Scilly museum, having been located and raised by a diver in 1964.

Another tragic loss close at hand was that of the Port Madoc brig *Criccieth Castle*, under-deck tonnage 233, built at Port Madoc by Morris Owen in 1876, which struck on the south-western corner of Peninnis between the Murrs and Inner Head on 9 February 1883. Bound from Fray Bentos to Liverpool via Falmouth with patent guano, she had received orders and left Carrick Roads on 2 February, only to strike Scilly and go down at night leaving no survivors from her crew of six. Three bodies were later found, those of the seventeen-year-old Santa Cruz cook, James Ruban, her master James Morris of Barmouth, and a Falmouth pilot. Identification of the wreck was made from a lifebelt marked 'CC. Port

Madoc', some papers found floating, and timbers strewn the width of Porth Cressa beach. A considerable amount of wreckage still lies on the seabed hard up against the steep cliff-face between the Murrs and The Chair, and although it has not been possible to identify them with certainty. a number of items raised by divers in 1964, including sounding leads, copper hull fastenings, brass fittings and an anchor, probably came from this particular wreck. A more modern vessel, the Swansea steam trawler *Roche Castle*, also struck Peninnis on 14 April 1911 in fog. Loaded with thirty tons of fish from Morocco for Hull, she was refloated and taken into port the following morning.

At the mouth of Porthcressa lies an outcrop known as Nicholls Rocks, which took their name from the master of a vessel, bound from Scilly to Harve de Grace with wheat, which was blown ashore here and lost on 28 April 1738.[4] An earlier wreck still unidentified, under Morning Point, the location of the sewer outfall for St Mary's, left a number of iron cannon scattered in the shallows, amongst which have been found many lead and iron ingots. A French lugger, the *Henri Letour*, Newport to Basac Indre, also went ashore in Porth Cressa Bay, but was towed off by pilots, as did the Whitehaven brigantine *Emily Burnyeat* in fog on 23 May 1873, while carrying copper ore from Lalasa for Swansea. Unsuccessful attempts were made by the tug *Guide* to tow her clear of the rocks the same day, but next morning she was hove off, only slightly damaged. Less than three months previously, her sister-ship, the *Sarah Burnyeat*, a Whitehaven barque, had gone aground in Porth Loo under Harrys Walls, the site of unfinished sixteenth-century harbour fortifications. On passage from Madras to London with cotton, hides and skins, the *Sarah Burnyeat* was ashore for two days before being refloated by

A Liverpool registered ship, the wooden *Minnehaha*, stranded and wrecked on Jolly rock, at the base of Peninnis, 18 January 1874, Captain, pilot and eight crew members were drowned.

the *Queen of the Bay*. In 1880, a ship's name-board bearing the word *Voltri* in gilt lettering on a blue background was found on Porth Cressa beach one morning and was assumed to have come from a wreck. Gigs carried out a search of the islands, but nothing more was ever found. On New Year's Eve the following year a particularly bad south-westerly gale caused the anchor cables of the French brigantine *Minerve* of St Malo to part and she drove ashore. Her seven crew were all saved, six by the local LSA crew and one by boat. By morning the vessel, bound from Swansea to Cadiz with coal, had gone to pieces on the rocks of Morning Point.

Going back to Old Town Bay, the long stretch of coast on the north side between Church Point and Porth Minick, holds not only the remains of many small sailing ships but also the rusting plates of the steamer *Brodfield*. Owned by the Brodfield Steamship Co of Holland House, London, this 3,567 tons register ship sailed from Le Havre for Barry in ballast on 11 November 1916 with a crew of seventy and Capt. Hubert Rowland of Birkenhead in command. Though the German U-Boat campaign was at its peak, she sailed alone, following a route recommended by the local naval authorities, and was making the best speed of which she was capable until fog off Start Point dictated a reduction to seven knots. Shortly after dark, soundings were taken and showed forty-two fathoms with a sandy bottom; a second set at midnight showed forty-nine fathoms. At 2.50 am on 13 November the fog thickened and speed was further reduced, the ship's siren continuing to blare out its mournful dirge. On the bridge were the captain and the second mate, whilst a seaman had been posted in the crow's nest on the foremast and two apprentices on the forecastle head, it being the latter who first sighted the cliffs dead ahead. Although their warning shout came in time to have the engines put to full-astern, it was too late to stop the ship striking heavily and grounding on the rocks beneath Blue Carn.

Boats were lowered and the crew mustered, while the carpenter went round sounding the double-bottom tanks, finding the forepeak and No 1 hold leaking badly and slowly filling. Soundings around the hull showed five fathoms opposite the damaged hold and fifteen astern. A radio message was sent asking for immediate assistance from tugs, after which the tank-tops on Nos 3 and 4 holds were removed so that they could be flooded to counterbalance the bow section and lift the ship clear of the rocks. By 6 am the fog had lifted, and at 7.30, on the top of the tide, the engines were started in an attempt to pull the ship off. As the water boiled around her thrashing propeller, she began to swing slowly to port, and when a hastily-rigged kedge anchor failed to check the swing, the *Brodfield* ended up broadside on to the shore, bumping heavily in the surf. At 8 am several naval patrol vessels arrived on the scene and attempted a tow, but without success, and even later, after assistance from five other ships and her own engines, she still remained fast ashore. A salvage crew then arrived and worked on her for three days until a gale sprang up and forced them to leave. The gale freshened rapidly and during the night of 16-17 November the *Brodfield* broke in two and became a total loss. A steel-hulled, schooner-rigged steamship, she had been built at Hawthorn Leslie's yard at Hebburn in 1899 as the *Surrey*, then sold to the Blue Star Line and renamed in 1915. At the enquiry held on 17 November, the captain was cleared of all blame, the stranding being attributed to bad visibility as the result of fog.

Continuing east towards Porth Hellick Point, Porth Loggos is known to have been the scene of the wreck in 1771 of an unidentified ship carrying a cargo of salt. Wreckers got to work on her and the authorities were hard pressed to stop looting. Later, one of her anchors was found half a mile away, buried under some stones on Salakee Downs. There is also evidence to support the story of another, larger shipwreck in the vicinity, since two enormous iron anchors, their wooden stocks long since eaten through, lie embedded in the sand bottom between Church Porth and Newfoundland Point. Even so, two anchors do not necessarily mean a wreck, and these may have simply been abandoned in some long-

One of two steamships wrecked due to fog during the same night, the London registered *Lady Charlotte* lies half submerged on the rocks at Porth Hellick, 11 May 1917. Her coal cargo is still being salvaged to this day.

forgotten incident. The quiet sheltered waters of Porth Hellick, where the body of Sir Clowdisley Shovell came ashore and was buried in 1707, may seem remote from such disasters but, in fact, they hide the remains of a large steamer, the *Lady Charlotte*, and it was here, too, that the French brig *Nerina* came ashore in 1840, upside down, with three men and a boy still alive inside her hull.

The 114-ton *Nerina* of Dunkirk had sailed from her home port on 31 October 1840, commanded by Capt. Pierre Everaert. She was bound for Marseilles with a cargo of canvas and oil, and carried a crew of six in addition to the captain's 14-year-old nephew, Nicholas Nissen. During the early hours of Monday, 16 November, a gale forced her to heave-to about thirty miles south-west of Scilly. Four hours later, still carrying only a close-reefed main topsail and mainsail, she was struck by a very large sea and turned completely over. Only one man was on deck at the time, a seaman named Bourneard, who disappeared; inside the fore-castle, two seamen, Vincent and Vantire, were able to grasp the windlass bitts, draw them-selves up to the keelson and keep their heads

above water. A third man with them, Jeanne Marie, somehow got entangled and drowned after thrashing about violently for a time. In the capsize, the cargo had fallen towards the inverted deckhead, distorting the bulkhead between forecastle and hold, so that Vincent and Vantire were able to work their way aft the length of the vessel, towards the sound of voices.

Capt. Everaert, the mate Jean Gallo, and young Nicholas were all aft in the cabin when the ship turned turtle and were trapped inside. The mate opened a hatch in the deck, cleared out some empty casks and they were able to scramble into the narrow space, where they were joined shortly afterwards by the two seamen. There was no light in their shallow prison other than that reflected dimly through the sea and cabin skylight and, forced to sit waist-deep in water with necks bent, their only relief was to take it in turns to stretch full length and relieve cramped and frozen limbs. For two days they endured this awful torture, without food or water, and seeking to quench their thirst by chewing bark from the casks. As time wore on and the air became more foul they were threatened by suffocation, and the mate, who had been working on the hull with a knife, re-doubled his efforts to make a hole. Fortunately, the blade broke before he could succeed, as otherwise the trapped air would have escaped and the vessel would have sunk.

During the night of Wednesday, 18 November, it came on to blow, and the inverted hull was tossed about. Vincent, caught by an upsurge, fell through the cabin hatch and was drowned, whilst the remainder scrambled towards the bow. Shortly afterwards, it was noticed that the water level had fallen, then rocks were seen underwater through the cabin roof and the *Nerina* became fast on shore. Unbeknown to the survivors, the brig had drifted ashore at Porth Hellick about midnight, and lay there until 7 am on the Thursday, when an islander found her high and dry. Approaching the hull, he pushed his hand through a hole in one quarter and was terrified when he felt it grasped and held firm from the inside. Local farmers cut her hull open with axes and liberated the survivors who had by then been trapped inside for three days and nights.

Later, it was learnt that the *Nerina* had in fact, been sighted about a mile offshore on the previous afternoon, and been taken in tow by two pilot-boats. But the lines had parted in the rough seas and she had been abandoned with little more than her keel showing. Had the wreck not been taken in tow and brought that much closer to the islands, the ebb tide would almost certainly have carried it out into the Atlantic.

The other wreck incident connected with Porth Hellick concerned the 3,593 tons gross steamer *Lady Charlotte* of London. Carrying coal from Cardiff to Alexandria, she went ashore in dense fog only a matter of hours before the *Italia* struck the Wingletang on 11 May 1917. Owned by the Redcroft Steam Navigation Co of Newcastle, the *Lady Charlotte* had originally been the *Aphrodite*, built by the Tyne Iron Steamboat Co in 1905. Two small steamships on Admiralty Fleet Messenger Service, ship numbers 30 and 38, thought to have been lost off Porth Hellick on 31 July 1917, were in fact sunk by U-Boat gunfire well offshore. The 486 ton *Turquoise* of Glasgow, acting on sealed orders, was 60 miles south-west of Bishop rock when attacked at 4pm without warning. Abandoned immediately, she sank fifteen minutes later, her chief-engineer killed by gunfire, and two seamen wounded. The smaller, 405 ton *Nugget*, also of and from Glasgow, was ordered to stop fifteen miles further north-east, probably by the same U-Boat, at 7.30pm. Turning on her attacker, the *Nugget* attempted unsuccessfully to ram her opponent, but after fifteen shells had been fired into her hull the crew also abandoned ship, being picked up by the Dutch sailing vessel *Annetta*, landing at St Mary's the following day.

Pelistry Bay, sheltering behind Tolls Island, saw the wreck of the French chassemarée *Frère et Soeur*, driven ashore by the same blizzard that sent the Padstow smack *Porth* on to the rocks at St Agnes in March 1891. Of the five Frenchmen aboard, only the master and his brother, the mate, were saved. Further north, a 15-ton wooden cutter named *St Christophe* of Camaret, France, was lost on Innisidgen on 16 October 1907, her crew of five landing safely, while on 16 October 1820 the American ship *City of Edinburgh*, from St Johns, New Brunswick, to London, dragged her anchors from the lee of Samson island and drifted over to Little Crow Rock. Badly damaged by the high seas, she fell over onto her side and would have been lost but for the local pilots who managed to warp her to the 'pool' three days later. The brig *Rosherville* of London, bound for Jamaica, Brabyn master, was at anchor in the roads discharging some of her cargo of rice, beer, wine and brandy, when, at 5 pm on 3 March 1855, she caught fire, burnt her hawser through and drifted ashore at Pendrathen, near Bar Point. Most of her crew were ashore at the time and by the following day the tide had

extinguished the flames, leaving only a gutted hulk.

Creeb Rock and Carn Moval Point have been the setting for several incidents, usually involving vessels which dragged their anchors in the 'pool' or St Mary's Roads. The French brig *La Maria Clara*, which was carrying timber when captured and taken prize by a Jersey privateer, went ashore on Carn Morval on 30 December 1780, and the *Letitia Tennant* of Stromness, Limerick to London, finished up on the Creeb on 14 April 1829. The following February, a Dutch barque, the *Borodino*, Haines master, carrying oil, oak, ivory and gold-dust from Sierra Leone to Milford, dragged onto Carn Morval windbound in the roads. An unidentified transport vessel on passage from Boston to Portsmouth with wounded soldiers also dragged and went ashore on Taylors Island on 4 December 1777, and a French prize-ship followed her in 1793. Taylors Island also saw the two-funnelled Scilly packet steamer *Lyonesse* ashore during thick fog

An unusual double-ended paddle-steamer, the Liverpool owned *GEM* was on passage to Africa with coal, when her cable parted in St Mary's Pool on 21 November 1881 and she stranded at Porth Loo to become a total wreck.

on 22 June 1900, but she was more fortunate than most and was off again that same day.

From here the coastline of St Mary's swings into Porthloo, Porthmellin and finally Hugh Town harbour, a natural anchorage that is officially known as St Mary's Pool. Its use is now restricted almost entirely to movements of the current passenger/cargo ferry RMV *Scillonian III*, which uses the port on a daily basis in the summer season, the cargo ship MV *Gry Maritha* and local and visiting small craft, but it was once a busy and thriving port. Ships from the far corners of the world then lay at anchor here, or discharged cargo alongside the old quay built by Godolphin, or the more modern extension started by the Duke of Leeds and completed by Augustus Smith, or 'Emperor' Smith as he was known locally. Four shipyards operated on the towns two beaches from the 1830s, until killed off by a lack of orders for wooden vessels, and their inability to build with iron. At first, locally-built vessels rarely exceeded sixty tons, mostly schooners and sloops which were used extensively in the Mediterranean trade, bringing back fruit from Africa, the Azores and Portugal. By 1839 there were twenty sizeable ships registered at St Mary's, all engaged in foreign trade, and the great boom in shipbuilding that followed saw vessels of 300 tons or more on local slip-ways. Porthcressa also had its yards, the last vessel to be launched there being the *David Auterson* on 12 September 1870, which only the following day went aground in Grimsby Channel, fortunately with only slight damage to her hull sheathing. The Hugh Town yards managed to survive until the early 1880s and closed only after completing two smacks for the east coast trade, the *Fortuna* and the *Queen of the Isles*.

The beach and sandy shallows of Porth Loo are deceptive, and whilst one might imagine any vessel driven ashore here would stand every chance of being saved, in fact several have become total, wrecks. A 400-ton West Indiaman, the *Melantho*, Richard Hardie master, went ashore here early in February 1801 and was saved, the only casualty being her 23-year-old captain who drowned after falling from a rock. The French barque *Ticina*, with a cargo of oil and nuts, became a total loss on the beach in 1869, and another French barque, the *Express* of Marseilles, on 15 December that same year. Her cargo of pistachio nuts from Rio Congo for Caen was salvaged but the vessel herself was a loss. A double-ended paddle-steamer of Liverpool, the *Gem*, owned by John Lander of Birkenhead, was another victim of Porth Loo. Although only a very small ship, being only 118 tons gross, she was on passage from Holyhead for the Brass River, in Africa, with thirty-seven tons of coal as ballast. Her master was George Gibson and she carried a crew of fourteen. A serious leak was discovered on 31 October 1881, and she was beached at St Ives on the north coast of Cornwall for examination. Finally, 21 November found her moor-

ed to a buoy in St Mary's 'pool' but the cable parted during the night and she drifted ashore to become a total loss.

The closing days of November 1863 saw a sudden deterioration in the weather conditions, which brought some 500 sailing ships into St Mary's Roads for shelter. Amongst them was the 662 tons gross tea clipper *Friar Tuck* of Liverpool, which arrived on the 27th of the month from Foo-Chow-Foo with a full cargo of tea, two of her masts sprung and the body of the ship's carpenter, who had recently died at sea. By the last day of November the elements had erupted into a hurricane from the north-west that left a trail of havoc throughout the country, and saw six vessels wrecked or in distress in Scilly alone. These were the *Friar Tuck*; the *Euphemie*, Cardiff to Nantes with coal, sunk by accident in shallow water; the *Adolphe*, also with coal for Nantes, sunk by collision in St Helens Pool; the Falmouth schooner *Oscar*, ashore on St Helens; and the brigs *Diana* and *Lavinia* ashore on Rat Island, the former being subsequently refloated.

The *Friar Tuck* parted her cables and went ashore on Newfort Island at the height of the storm on 2 December, her master, Capt. Fordyce, ordering her masts to be cut away. A rocket line was fired across the wreck from ashore and the crew of twenty-two rescued. Salvage work was started as soon as the weather moderated, and three small shiploads of tea, in addition to spars, sails, hawsers and ship's stores, were sent to London. The islanders, however, were not going to miss the opportunity of a little something from the sea for themselves and large quantities of the tea found its way into local hands. Launched at Aberdeen in 1857 and owned by J. Beasley of Red Cross Street, Liverpool, the *Friar Tuck* had been a very profitable ship for her owners, having made a gross profit of £12,389 over her last six voyages. Many years later, in November 1943, a flat-bottomed assault vessel belonging to a different age, *Landing Craft Tank No 354*, went ashore in exactly the same spot but survived to take an active part in the D-Day landings in Normandy.

Porth Mellin has seen a large number of sailing ships ashore, the majority of which were got off, but some became total losses, including the brig *New York* of London, William Baker master, in 1782. On passage from London to Antigua with pork, beef and biscuit, she was wrecked while attempting to leave the harbour. An Aberystwyth schooner, the *Naomi*, parted her cables in the 'pool' and went ashore on 1 November 1859 but, almost incredibly, was successfully warped the 700 yd necessary to get her afloat again and so was saved. The brigantine *Skulda* of Sweden put into Scilly on 4 October 1864, discharged cargo and effected repairs, but on leaving on 26 November was driven ashore and lost. In 1885, the cutter *Lurline* of Jersey was put onto the beach on 5 November, and on 18 October 1886 the *Harriet*, a Bristol coasting schooner, broke from her moorings alongside the old quay and drove ashore on Porth Mellon, but was saved. A French lobster ketch, the *Guiding Star*, parted her cables after being fouled by the steam-trawler *St Clyde* whilst at anchor on 1 September 1908. She fetched up on Porth Mellon beach along with the crabbers *Fils De L'Humanite*, *Souf Frances* and *L'Etoile Polaire*, all of which were successfully refloated on 8 September. Carn Thomas, the location of the

St Mary's lifeboat station, saw a sloop on the rocks on 23 October 1820; the revenue cutter *Providence* on 11 August 1852; a schooner, *Symmetry*, from Gloucester on 4 February 1840, and the *Mary & Eliza*, a London schooner, Tregarthen master, on 9 October 1844. The *Mary & Eliza* was carrying smoked herrings from her home port to Cadiz and Gibraltar and her crew were rescued by Dennett's rocket apparatus its first recorded use at Scilly. After her wreck had gone to pieces on the rocks, the remains were sold for £9 10s. Yet another wreck in the 'pool' area was the *Janus* of North Shields on 14 February 1825.

When the original Hugh Town jetty was extended, it was taken out to and beyond Rat Island, a large outcrop originally named after its rodent population. Leyland's description of Rat Island reads: 'there is one isles of the Scylles cawled Rat Island, yn which be so many rattes that, yf a horse or any other lyving best be brought thyther, they devore hym.'[5] The rats have long since disappeared, and the only total wreck to occur here was the locally-owned *Kitty O'Flanaghan*, a schooner, on 14 February

LCT 354 (Landing Craft (Tank)), driven ashore during a gale on Newford Island, St Mary's, 1943, later refloated and used in the D-Day landings on the Normandy coast.

1838, although there have been minor incidents, such as the brig *Lavinia*, or the *Diana*, Quebec to Southampton with timber, which went ashore during the *Friar Tuck* hurricane on 1 December 1863. After her mast had been cut away and other dismantling had taken place, she was brought alongside the jetty on 8 December. The *Mary Roberts* also managed to get herself clear after grounding on Bacon Ledges on 19 October 1888, but a 1-ton wooden cutter, the *Viking,* which went ashore here on 10 March 1905 was wrecked with the loss of one life. The packet-steamer *Scillonian* was very nearly another victim on 5 August 1932, but succeeded in warping herself free with the aid of her kedge anchor after only one and a half hours aground.

Although re-location of the wreck sites of the *Association* and *Eagle* with their gold and silver excited the imagination of those interested in treasure hunting, an even greater prize remained undiscovered amongst the Western Rocks until 1971. The evidence had long been in print; Lt Robert Heath, a military officer in the Garrison of St Mary's in his *Account of the Islands of Scilly*, published in 1750 wrote:

> About the year 1743, a Dutch East Indiaman, outward bound was lost off St Ages in about twenty or twenty-two fathoms of water, with all the people. Their firing of guns, as a signal of distress, was heard in the night; but none could give them assistance. Many of their bodies floated ashore at St Mary's and other islands, where they were buried by the inhabitants, and some were taken up floating upon the tide and buried. A Dutch lady with her children, and servants, going to her husband, and East India Governor, was prevented seeing of him by this unhappy accident. A diver thereupon was sent, by the Dutch merchants, to discover and weigh the plate of considerable value. But the tide running strong at bottom, and the sea appearing thick, the diver could not see distinctly through the glass of his engine so returned without success. This wreck

remains as a booty for those who can find it.

It is quite remarkable that Heath, writing the above account only seven years after the event, was seemingly unaware of the ship's name, or the date of the wreck. The ship was in fact the *Hollandia*, Captain Jan Kelder, which sank on her maiden voyage, on 3 July 1743, with the loss of all on board – 276 crew, passengers and troops, plus a valuable general cargo of lead and trade goods, as well as military stores and silver specie. Heath stated that she had been lost off St Agnes, whereas the Rev Woodley insisted she struck the Gunners and sank nearby [7], both in fact proved almost correct. However, there was also a third reference, implying that the 'mystery' Dutchman sank much closer to St Mary's, which reads:

> We spread our sails to the wind and ran gaily through St Mary's Pool, a little further on is the rock on which the Dutch East Indiaman struck and went to pieces with 250,000 in silver guilders, many of which have been and still are, picked up [8].

On possible explanation is that the author of this reference mixed up the Indiaman wreck with that of the *Triumph* on the Steval in 1736, although her specie was gold, not silver which was literally, found in the shallows.

Whilst tens of thousands of people must have read Heath's account of the wreck, only Rex Cowan, assisted by his wife Zeldie, believed in it sufficiently to research the incident in the Hague archives of the Netherlands, and ultimately to locate and salvage that vast treasure. Possibly the most unlikely candidate to become a wreck-hunter, Rex Cowan was at the time a solicitor in a London practice, with no professional sea experience, had never been involved with shipwreck before, and was not a diver. To his credit, he never once gave up the long and expensive search which he funded over the best part of three years, the first of his successful projects. In point of fact, the team's metal detecting magnetometer sensor or 'fish'

passed over the *Hollandia* site in 1969/70 but the signal trace was considered too small to be a wreck. After failing to find the wreck over a long period, a re-run over all the minor targets on 16 September 1971 gave a pronounced reading in the vicinity of George Peter's Ledge, west of Annet. A diver went down, and the elusive Dutch East Indiaman was found, which more than justified Heath's comment, 'This wreck remains a booty for those who can find it'. A display of material from the *Hollandia* can be seen in the Isles of Scilly Museum in Hugh Town.

Offshore from the Star Castle in a north-westerly direction can be found Woodcocks Ledge, where the Fowey brig *Thomas*, Edward Nicholls master, after sinking in seven fathoms during a south-easter on 23 February 1833, was subsequently weighed and beached on 11 June. Closer inshore, the rocky outcrop known as the Barrel of Butter claimed the *Indipendenza* of Recco, a Genoan barque, in 1881. Her loss can be attributed indirectly to the Crim Rocks,

The team involved in the successful relocation of the Dutch East Indiaman *Hollandia* (1743), examine some of the pillar-dollar and ducatoon coins they recovered in 1971/2. Left to right: Terry Hiron (seated), 'Chippy' Pearce, Jack Gayton, Rex Cowan (Team leader), Jim Heslin, David Stedeford (boatman).

Overleaf: Despite giving the appearance of a luxury steam yacht, the SS *Serica* was carrying a cargo of coal when wrecked on an uncharted rock near the Woolpack Beacon, St Mary's, 24 November 1893.

since having hit rocks elsewhere she struck again at 3pm on 24 September during fog. Steering south-south-east under plain sail, her pilot, William Ouzman, thought his charge was safely south-west of Scilly by at least fifteen miles. No observations had been possible since leaving Lundy due to the weather, but soundings had been taken regularly, and had shown an average depth of between forty-two and forty-eight fathoms. Minutes later, breakers were sighted ahead and the barque struck heavily four times in quick succession. She was hauled off but struck yet again, this time

remaining fast on the rocks for about five minutes during which time the water level in the hold rose to 6 ft. When she had floated clear, her master, Fillipo Caffarena, bore up for Scilly through Broad Sound heading towards the roads, but she leaked so badly that the crew of fourteen were soon forced to abandon her. After rowing around within sight of the ship for some time and deciding that she was not going to sink after all, the crew re-boarded but, not liking what they found, disembarked for the second time and rowed alongside their ship as she slowly drifted down on to the shore and was wrecked. Her cargo of 1,200 tons of hides, horn and guano spilled out, and the ship being in a difficult position for salvage, most of it was lost on the tide, St Mary's Pool being thick with horns at one stage.

Not far from the Barrel of Butter can be found the Steval Rock, notorious for the wreck of the richly-laden *Triumph* which went ashore during a storm on 9 October 1736. Bound from Jamaica to London with rum, sugar and dye-wood, she carried in addition £10,000 in

St Mary's lifeboat RNLI *Elsie* standing by the Lowestoft steam trawler *Lord Haldane* (LT. 1141) on 20 March 1929, after going ashore near the Steval, Garrison shore, St Mary's.

gold coins, which was scattered amongst the rocks of Garrison shore.[8] Her captain, bo'sun, carpenter and several seamen were drowned after jumping into the sea, while those who remained on board, including the mate and the surgeon, were saved. A far more fortunate encounter here was that of a mackerel-laden steam-trawler, the 91 tons gross *Lord Haldane* of Lowestoft, owned by the Lowestoft Steam Herring Drifter Co, which went ashore on 20 March 1929 and was towed off by the St Mary's lifeboat.

Close to Conger Ledge, and well inshore of the wreck symbol shown on Admiralty chart No 883, can be found the remains of a very old steam tug, the 283 tons gross *Blazer*, (ex-*Charm*) of Liverpool, built by S. M. Knight of Ayr in 1888. She sank on 10 November 1918 and became notorious locally in 1966 when divers found live ammunition on board. The Garrison shore has seen innumerable wrecks including the *Mecurius*, Esink master, a large Dutch East Indiaman on 19 January 1835, whilst amongst those fortunate enough to be saved were the *Good Intent*, Lefevre master, Waterford to Lisbon, aground on the Woolpack on 6 March 1809; the schooner *Vesper* also on the Woolpack on 1 May 1844 and the

ketch *Charles Francis* of Scilly, owned by William Mumford but registered at Plymouth, which struck but later floated off on 23 February 1898.

The wooden ketch *Charles Francis*, owned by William Mumford in Scilly, but registered at Plymouth, was being used as a collier when she stranded on the Garrison shore, near the Newman, 23 February 1898.

The final wreck incident in this chapter, although dozens have perforce been omitted, must be the *Serica*, a particularly fine, steel screw, schooner-rigged steamer of 1,736 tons register Her last voyage began at Cardiff on 16 November 1893, when she sailed for Port Said with a crew of twenty-five and a cargo of coal. Bad weather was encountered the following day when off Hartland Point, and by dawn on the 18th the *Serica* was in trouble when the storm ripped the tarpaulin covers from off Nos 3 and 4 holds, flooded the main cabin and swept away everything that was movable abaft the bridge. Her captain, Sydney Smith, had a remarkable escape in that he was washed clean overboard twice, and twice was flung back aboard by the sea. The *Serica* eventually reached Scilly on the 19th in a very distressed condition with pumps choked, serious damage on deck, and a heavy list. To quote the words of the local Receiver of Wreck at the time, 'the only wonder is that the vessel kept afloat'.[9] On 24 November, the *Serica* left St Mary's at low water to continue her voyage, but struck a rock and had to be run ashore 150 yd north-north-west of the Woolpack beacon. She was abandoned almost immediately and only minor salvage was ever carried out on the wreck, all work ceasing on 3 January 1894. The rock the *Serica* struck was, in fact, marked as lying in eight fathoms but was later found to be in less than twenty-four feet. It's doubtful if it was any consolation to her owners, but that rock was given the name of the ship and today is marked on all charts as the Serica Rock.

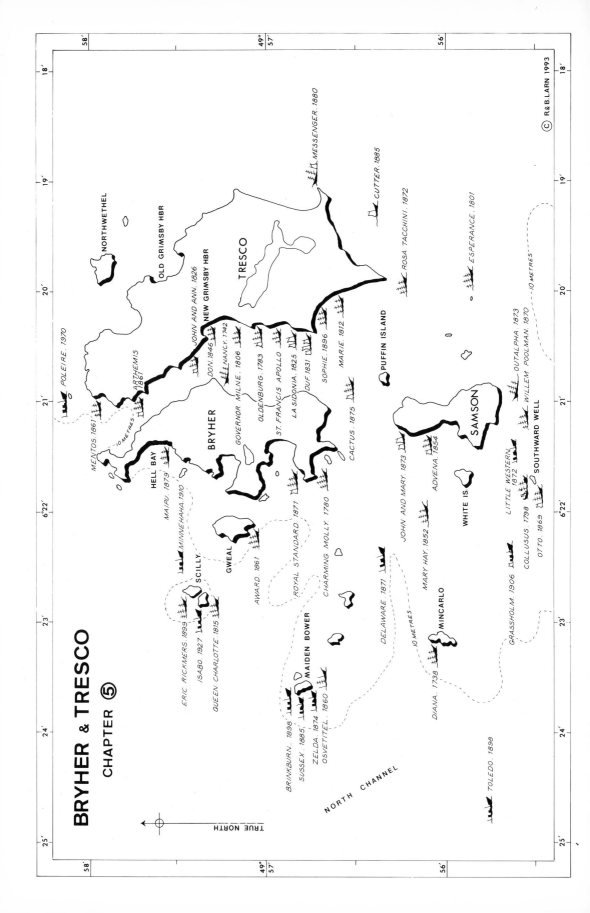

BRYHER & TRESCO

CHAPTER ⑤

TRUE NORTH

© R&B.LARN 1993

POLE IRE. 1970

NORTHWETHEL

OLD GRIMSBY HBR

NEW GRIMSBY HBR

TRESCO

JOHN AND ANN. 1826

MESSENGER. 1880

CUTTER. 1885

ROSA TACCHINI. 1872

ESPERANCE. 1801

MENTOS. 1861

ARTHEMIS 1867

10 METRES

DON. 1846

NANCY. 1742

OLDENBURG. 1783

GOVERNOR MILNE. 1806

ST. FRANCIS APOLLO

LA SIDONIA. 1825

DUF. 1831

SOPHIE. 1896

MARIE. 1812

CACTUS. 1875

PUFFIN ISLAND

BRYHER

HELL BAY

MAIPU. 1879

MINNEHAHA.1910

SCILLY

GWEAL

AWARD 1861

ROYAL STANDARD 1871

CHARMING MOLLY. 1780

ERIC RICKMERS. 1899

ISABO. 1927

QUEEN CHARLOTTE. 1815

BRINKBURN. 1898

SUSSEX. 1885

ZELDA. 1874

OSVETITEL. 1860

MAIDEN BOWER

DELAWARE 1871

10 METRES

DIANA. 1738

MINCARLO

JOHN AND MARY. 1873

ADVENA. 1864

MARY HAY. 1852

WHITE IS.

SAMSON

LITTLE WESTERN. 1872

OUTALPHA. 1873

WILLEM POOLMAN. 1870

COLLUSUS. 1798

OTTO. 1869

SOUTHWARD WELL

10 METRES

GRASSHOLM. 1906

TOLEDO. 1898

NORTH CHANNEL

5

Bryher, Samson and Tresco Islands

ONE mile north-west of Hugh Town, across St Mary's Roads, lie three islands, Samson, Bryher and Tresco which, with their outlying rock formations, form the most picturesque area in the whole of Scilly. They have an atmosphere and geography peculiar to themselves and 'Fairy Tale Bryher' and 'Tropical Tresco'[1] are but two of the romantic titles which have been bestowed on them. Surrounded by rocks and ledges almost as numerous as those of the Western Rocks, they abound in such descriptive or obscure names as Roaring Ledge, Buccabu, Illiswilgig, Stinking Porth, Hell Bay and Tobaccoman's Ledge. The area has seen its share of sunken ships and drowned seamen, but despite the dangers of the surrounding rocks the number of wrecks is remarkably low in comparison with the Western Rocks or St Agnes.

Offshore to the south of Samson, which is now an uninhabited island, a shallow reef known as Southward Well was the site of one of the most famous wrecks on Scilly, that of HMS *Colossus*, which went ashore on 10 December 1798, fortunately with the loss of only one life. Commanded by Capt. George Murray, the *Colossus* was a 3rd rate, 74-gun ship-of-the-line of 1,703 tons(bm), built by Clevely at Gravesend and launched on 4 April 1787. She had been in the Mediterranean for almost two years when ordered home, during which time she had seen considerable service, taking part in the Battle of Cape St Vincent, patrolling off Cadiz and Lisbon, and assisting in the blockade of Malta. Long service abroad told heavily on these old 'wooden walls' of England, so that by November 1798, the *Colossus* had rotten sails, worn rigging. soft timbers and little or no spare gear, most of her stores having been removed to maintain and service other ships that were even worse off. She left Lisbon in charge of a convoy, arriving in St Mary's Roads on Friday, 7

December, with eight smaller vessels, to shelter from an unfavourable north-east wind.

Although poorly provisioned and unseaworthy, the *Colossus* carried far more men than her normal complement, having on board sick and wounded sailors from the Battle of the Nile. In addition, she was heavily laden with private stores, including a unique collection of Etruscan vases and paintings belonging to Sir William Hamilton. It was said 'there was scarcely an officer in Lord Nelson's fleet but had put on board the *Colossus* some presents for their friends, which had been taken on board the French fleet.'[2] It was rumoured after the wreck that she carried specie, but although this had been the intention, at the last moment Capt. Murray had refused to oblige the Lisbon merchants who had approached him. No doubt he would have been reluctant to decline the offer, since naval officers in those days made a practice of transporting large sums of money for merchant bankers. In return, they received as much as 5 per cent of the gross value, and vast personal fortunes were amassed in this manner, a senior officer receiving as much as £25,000 or more for one bullion shipment on what was after all, normal Crown service.

By the late afternoon of 10 December, the wind had swung to the south-east and increased to gale force. At 4 pm the main bower cable to which the *Colossus* was riding parted, and although a small bow and sheet anchor were lowered, they failed to take a hold and merely dragged over the sandy bottom. The watch on deck were sent aloft to strike the topmasts in order to reduce windage, but the ship continued to drag and at 8 pm struck the rocks. During the night, she lost her rudder and took in water so rapidly that she had to be abandoned at first light. The late afternoon of 11 December saw every man off the ship, including the sick and wounded, with only one casualty, a quartermaster who fell overboard while taking soundings and drowned. That night the warship fell over onto her beam ends and began to break up. A considerable amount of gear was salvaged including 'many useful pieces of masts, spars, copper and iron etc, a 75-cwt anchor and iron cannon'. One unusual item recovered was the embalmed body of Admiral Lord Shuldham in its lead cask which, disguised as a wooden crate, had been shipped as cargo, in deference to the seaman's superstition against carrying the dead aboard a ship at sea. On hearing of the wreck and the loss of his priceless art treasures, Sir William Hamilton reacted strongly: 'My phylosophy has been put to trial by the loss of the *Colossus*. You give me little hope, but I have learnt that the body insolvent of Admiral Shuldham has been saved from the wreck . . . damn his body, it can be of no use but to the worms, but my collection would have given information to the most learned.'[3] Some of the guns used in the garrison battery at St Mary's came from the wreck, salvaged and put back into service in 1852 after fifty-four years under water.

The wreck site of the *Colossus* was located and identified in 1974 by a team of divers led by Roland Morris. Amongst the iron carronades, shot, buttons, leather shoes and other personal artefacts, the team found and raised many thousands of sherds of Hamilton's famous pottery collection. Working closely with the British Museum, who loaned the sum of £40,000 to assist the excavation and concervation, all the sherds are now in the B.M.'s collection.

Southward Well has been the cause of many other wrecks and strandings, including the Swedish brigantine *Otto* laden with Stockholm tar and bound from Jacobstad to Bristol. On bringing up in St Mary's Roads, she parted both cables and after fouling the barque *Dorothy Thompson* drove ashore on 6 December 1869. Her crew were all saved, although several days later there was almost a casualty when they departed for the mainland aboard the Penzance packet. In bidding his crew a fond and no doubt alcoholic farewell, the *Otto's*

captain fell off the end of the Hugh Town jetty and almost drowned! Only thirty-six barrels of her cargo were saved before she broke up. In 1870, on 27 January. the ship *Willem Poolman* of Rotterdam went on the rocks here while on passage from Batavia to her home port but, assisted by local boatmen and pilots, plus a steamer, got off and both the ship and her cargo of coffee and tin were saved. The full-rigged ship *Outalpha* of London, on entering St Mary's Roads for shelter on 1 February 1873, touched bottom and remained fast in a dangerous position until refloated on the following tide. Bound from Adelaide to London with grain, she was one of fifty or so ships sheltering from a hurricane which swung from south-east to north within an hour.

Several incidents have already been mentioned concerning Scilly packets in trouble around the islands, and over the years two have become total wrecks, both in the same year, and one on the same rocks that claimed the *Colossus*. At 10.30 am on 5 October 1872, the West Cornwall Steamship Company's iron screw packet *Little Western*, left Penzance for the Isles of Scilly. She arrived at St Mary's in mid-afternoon, but sailed shortly afterwards when news was received that a French brigantine, the *Jane*, laden with ore, had lost her foremast and main topmast and was in distress seven miles south-west of the Bishop light. Two cruising pilot-cutters were first upon the scene, and when Capt. Hicks (not Capt. Tregarthen as is so often misquoted) arrived with the *Little Western*, he was much annoyed to find his services were not required. He cruised around for some two hours in the hope that the French master might change his mind, then headed back for port, leaving Robert Tonkin, the mate, on deck. No specific instructions or course were given, the captain merely saying that they would 'keep down for St Mary's Sound'. When abeam of the Spanish Ledges, Capt. Hicks took the helm and steered the ship close to St Agnes, passing within 60 ft of the Bristolman Rock before heading up towards the roads. Midnight, with the weather fine and clear, saw the packet doing about four knots across the roads, with all hands on deck preparing to anchor for the night. No lookout had been posted, and when land was suddenly sighted dead ahead, it was too late to take avoiding action. Mate Tonkin ordered the engine to full astern, while the captain called for port helm, then changed his mind and ordered it to starboard, but all to no effect. The *Little Western* struck a full ship's length north and east of Southward Well and began to settle in four fathoms.

At the subsequent enquiry held at Penzance, there was a suggestion that Capt. Hicks had been drunk, and this allegation was supported by the steward who declared that he had consumed half a tumbler of brandy and water at 8 pm, a quantity of ale at about 9.30 pm, followed by more brandy. Although drunkenness was never proved, the captain was found guilty of unseamanlike behaviour and neglect in misjudging the distance of his ship off shore, and for entering an anchorage without posting lookouts. As a result, his master's certificate was suspended for six months. Captain Hicks had been at sea for twenty-one of his fifty-five years, commanding 150 different ships, and had once piloted the royal yacht with Queen Victoria aboard. But as a result of the *Little Western* disaster Augustus Smith banished him from the islands, and he never sailed out of Scilly again. Launched in 1858 by James Henderson & Sons of Renfrew, the *Little Western* was owned by T. J. Burton of St Mary's. She was a steamer of 115 tons gross, 67 net, and 115 ft overall in length. Brought to Penzance in 1859 specially for the Isles of Scilly service, she normally made three passages a week, plus excursions and salvage jobs when opportunity offered, and was only the second steam vessel to serve between Penzance and St Mary's. The first had been the *Scotia,* specially chartered for the work in 1858 by the same owners until the *Little Western* had been completed. On 14 November 1872, the wreck of the *Little Western* was sold for £120, and though the purchaser announced his intention of raising the ship intact on the next spring tide, this was never accomplished.

Great Minalto, a rock a few hundred yards to the west, almost terminated the career of the South Shields steam-trawler *Grassholm* on 21 August 1906. On passage to Cardiff laden with fish, she encountered fog and in attempting to reach the anchorage went ashore. Although badly damaged about the bows, her crew warped her off and she was lying at anchor, filling fast, when the St Mary's lifeboat *Henry Dundas* arrived alongside. The lifeboat coxswain was engaged to save the trawler, and towed her safely into the harbour.

Midway between Mincarlo and Samson lie the Bream Ledges on which the 225 tons register, wooden barque *Mary Hay* was lost on 13 April 1852. From Jamaica to London, and commanded by Capt. Hogg, she was entering Broad Sound from the north-west when she struck the Steeple Rock. There was a Scilly pilot on board at the time, but he was so busy pointing out the dangerous rocks to the master and reassuring him that all was well, that he failed to notice his own position. Two minutes after the pilot had gone below for a meal, having declined to eat it on deck, the barque struck heavily and at once began to take in water. With distress signals flying, she was eventually anchored near Samson, but after hours of pumping the *Mary Hay* gave one great belch, lurched, and fell over on her side. There were some thirty men on deck at the time, as well as others in boats moored alongside, and though several had lucky escapes, no lives were lost. The following day, forty-six puncheons of rum, two casks of lime-juice, 1,170 bags of pimento, ship's stores, gear and clothing were salvaged. Of the remaining cargo, all the sugar was ruined, and only the ebony, logwood, coconuts and fustic were sold with the wreck for £72 on 17 April. After the weather moderated, the barque was refloated and taken to St Mary's pier where she was broken up, her figurehead later joining others in the Valhalla.

Although not strictly relevant to this chapter, mention should perhaps be made of the *Toledo,* a Sunderland steamer of 2,843 tons gross which, on Saturday 20 August 1898, ripped her bottom open on the same pinnacle of Steeple

Rock that had claimed the *Mary Hay* forty-six years earlier. With a crew of twenty-eight commanded by Capt. John Wishart, the steamer carried a general cargo, mostly wheat and oil cake, consigned to Van Stanton & Co of Rotterdam from Galveston. It was late afternoon when the *Toledo* was suddenly engulfed in fog close to the Bishop, and only minutes later she struck the Steeple. Robert Ferrer, the second engineer on watch below when she struck, saw her boilers literally lift from their mountings. With her bottom plates ripped open from bow to engine-room, she filled at the rate of a foot a minute, and the crew barely had time to lower the boats and abandon ship before she rolled over and sank bow-first in twenty-five fathoms. Built by J. L. Thompson of Sunderland in 1882, and owned by J. Tully & Co, the *Toledo*, lying in the fairway with her masts only 18 ft below the surface, was considered a hazard to navigation, so divers were engaged to blow her up with explosives.

Mention the name *Delaware* to anyone in Scilly, and they will almost certainly link it with a rescue still considered by some as one of the bravest in the history of the islands. It began early on 20 December 1871, when Bryher pilots sighted a large screw steamer in distress, battling close inshore against a severe northwest gale. By noon, the wind strength had increased still more, forcing the labouring vessel between Mincarlo and Seal Rock, towards Tearing Ledges. Watching through their telescopes, the pilots on shore saw her crew hoist a jib only to have it blown away, a staysail following soon after. Beam-on to the swell and rolling heavily, the steamer disappeared under a huge wave to reappear seconds later denuded of her entire bridge structure. Another great wave then broke over her decks and she went down almost within seconds. From a vantage point on Samson Hill, at the south end of Bryher, five survivors were sighted in the sea; two were in a boat, another two on a spar and one clung to wreckage. Realising they would almost certainly be carried onto White Island, a mile south-south-west, the Bryher gig *Albion* was prepared for sea. The 30-ft boat,

weighing almost half a ton, had its six oars lashed across its beam, and twelve men carried it bodily for half a mile from the boathouse at Great Par across to Rushy Bay.

Patrick Trevellick, an acknowledged leader in this sort of situation, was chosen as coxswain, and the *Albion* set off for Samson manned by William and Stephen Woodcock, Thomas Bickford, John Webber, Richard Ellis, James Jenkins, John Jacob Jenkins, William Jenkins, and Samson Jenkins. After gaining the lee of the island, by which time the men were already soaked and exhausted, some of them landed and got ashore in time to see the boat containing survivors strike White Island, and its two occupants scramble to safety. Leaving Richard Ellis on North Hill to signal back to Bryher if more men were needed, the heavy gig was again man-handled overland, this time across the 92m isthmus between East and West Par. Hardly stopping to draw breath after their exertion, they re-launched the gig and with six men rowing and the others bailing for their lives, they battled their way through the mountainous seas towards White Island. And when, utterly exhausted, they at last reached the island and ran the gig up through the foaming surf, it was only to find that the two survivors had collected together a huge pile of stones as ammunition with which to defend themselves! They later told their rescuers that their captain had described the Scillonians as little better than savages, and that they could expect short shrift if they were ever wrecked there. After giving various articles of their own clothing to the two half-naked seamen, the gig's crew made a thorough search of the island before returning to Samson, where survivors and rescuers alike collapsed from exhaustion. Meanwhile, Richard Ellis had noted their plight and had signalled from North Hill for a second gig, the *March*, to come over to Samson.

The two men rescued from White Island, the only survivors from the wreck, proved to be chief mate McWinnie and third mate Jenkins of the 3,423 tons gross Liverpool steamer *Delaware*, of and from Liverpool for Calcutta via Suez, with a general cargo which included cottons, silks, sheet-lead, tin and stationery. Built at Ramsey, Isle of Man, in 1865, the steamer had been lengthened by 60 ft after building to 380 ft, but left with her original engine, so there had been much controversy as to whether or not she was under-powered. The day following the wreck, after the ship's officers had been cared for on Bryher, every available man on the island set about recovering cargo from the sea. It has been said that the *Albion's* crew received neither public thanks nor reward for their gallant rescue, but this is not so. True that they received no testimonials or certificates, but they certainly received a reward of £15 from the Royal National Lifeboat Institution—not overmuch, perhaps, for a rescue which is still remembered as an outstanding feat of human endurance.

There have been many other minor incidents in this immediate area, such as the *John and Mary*, a Truro schooner abandoned in February 1893 after she had parted her cables

and collided with a Greek brig in St Mary's Roads, but later found ashore on Samson, towed off and taken to New Grimsby; the *Diana* of Calais, carrying wool, ashore on Mincarlo in November 1738; and the Italian barque *Cactus,* on passage from Tripoli to Cardiff with esparto grass, which struck on the northern rocks at 11.0 pm on 11 August 1875 during fog. Boarded by pilots at daybreak, she was anchored off Mincarlo, then run ashore between Bryher and Samson half full of water on the 12th, and finally taken to St Mary's pierhead on the 13th. Another near casualty was the brig *Advena*, Holmes master, driven onto Samson by a southeaster on 3 January 1854, and saved only after her masts had been cut down to lighten her sufficiently to float off at

The salvage steamer *Hyaena* alongside at St Mary's, assisting to land a boiler she had salvaged from the wreck of the SS *Zelda*, which sank close to Maiden Bower on 16 April 1874. Steel rails, part of the *Zelda's* cargo, lie on the quayside.

high-water. Peaked Rock, at the north-eastern corner of North Channel, brought about the loss of the steamer *Empire* of London, George Woodcock master. The 409-ton wooden vessel attempted to get into Scilly without a pilot during a severe gale, struck and sank in 20m on 26 November 1860.

The most seaward rock in this sector is the redoubtable Maiden Bower, so that it is not surprising that at least one large barque, three steamers and numerous small craft have come to grief here. The largest of the sailing ships was Austrian, the *Osvetitel*, Meilicich master, carrying barley from Ibrail to Falmouth. Thick fog blanketed the outline of Maiden Bower on 14 July 1860 when she went ashore to become a total wreck, about 1,000 quarters of her cargo being saved before she broke up.

The first steamer to be lost here was the *Zelda* and again fog was the contributory cause. It was a little after midnight on 16 April 1874 when the *Zelda's* siren broke the silence of Bryher, and two local gigs were the first to find the 1,300 tons gross, iron vessel hard and fast on the rocks. To say her career had been a short one would be a gross understatement, since she was less than thirty-two hours out on her maiden voyage! Owned by Glynn & Co of Liverpool, and bound from Liverpool to Palermo with a crew of thirty, two passengers and a general cargo, the *Zelda* was abandoned without loss of life only a short while before she parted amidships, her bow section sinking in ten fathoms, the stern in five. Her luckless master, Capt. Peace, was exonerated from any blame for the loss of his ship by the court of enquiry, and almost all the *Zelda's* valuable cargo was salvaged by divers who worked on the wreck for many weeks. A contemporary newspaper report listed the following goods as having been recovered: numerous cases of cotton goods, 208 cases of lard, 32 firkins of lard, 22 barrels of oil, 12 cakes of copper, 2 cases of copper-bottoms, 4 cases of sheet copper, 3 cases of yellow metal, 10 cases of soda-nitrate, 11 barrels of solder, 29 blocks of tin, frames of felt material, 100 tons of steel rail, cases of machinery, hogsheads of cotton

and other items. Some of the spoiled rice was sold off at Scilly and Penzance, but the bulk was shipped to Liverpool. For their services in rescuing the crew and passengers, the crews of the two gigs who had towed ashore two of the ship's boats, holding thirty persons in all, were each awarded £50.

Sister ship to the *Suffolk* and *Surrey*, the *Sussex* was another victim of Maiden Bower in 1885. These three ships maintained a regular service between London and Baltimore during the early 1880s, and although owned by three individual shipping companies, they were jointly managed by Hooper, Murrell & Williams Ltd of London. The *Surrey* was extensively damaged in collision off the Bishop Rock with the German ship *Uranus* on 4 January 1884, the *Sussex* totally wrecked at Scilly on 17 December 1885 and the *Suffolk* at the Lizard less than a year later on 28 September 1886. As with the *Zelda*, the deep-throated bellow of the *Sussex's* siren brought out the gigs from Bryher at dawn, although the vessel had, in fact, gone ashore some six hours earlier. Fifteen days out from Baltimore with a general cargo which included a great variety of Christmas fare and 250 head of cattle, the *Sussex* of London, with a crew of forty-five including seven cattlemen, had been navigated on dead reckoning for the last two days. Despite thick fog her master, Capt. Robert Robinson, had been pressing on at normal cruising speed and without stopping to take soundings, so it is hardly surprising that there was only a matter of seconds between the lookout's cry of 'breakers ahead' and the ship crashing on to rocks. The outcrop was the Seal Rock; so violent was the impact that the watch below were hurled from their bunks, and scrambled up on deck to find the four lifeboats already being lowered. Within five minutes, the portside plates of the engine-room collapsed, the depth of water inside the ship reached 18 ft and she began to settle fast. After taking to the boats, the crew suffered considerably from cold and exposure, since most were dressed either for the engine-room or their bunks. When, finally, the Bryher boats arrived, those who had abandoned the steamer returned to collect the

others and to retrieve papers, instruments and personal effects before landing on Bryher, and eventually St Mary's. With her stern completely submerged and the seas breaking over her bridge, the *Sussex* showed every sign of disintegrating. During the night of 4-5 January, she broke up completely and disappeared, after which timber and sacks of flour began drifting to the surface. Launched by Wigham, Richardson Ltd of Newcastle in March 1883, the 2,795 tons gross, three-masted *Sussex* was fitted with a two-cylinder, 275 nhp engine made by the same firm.

Twenty-four years after the *Zelda* went down, her rusting plates were joined by those of another steamer, the 3,229 tons gross, four-year-old *Brinkburn*, which struck and sank in fog on 15 December 1898 in similar circumstances. Bound from Galveston to Le Havre with 8,895 bales of cotton and 6,720 bags of cotton seed, she struck the Maiden Bower and

Carrying a large quantity of cotton and cotton seed, the steamship *Brinkburn* struck the Maiden Bower, off Bryher, on 15 December 1898 to become a total loss.

Overleaf: Minnehaha stranded on the Scilly rock, 18 April 1910.

was unable to get clear. Her crew, mostly Lascars, took to the boats and remained close to the wreck until daybreak, when once again the Bryher gigs were used to tow the survivors' boats ashore. The Liverpool Salvage Co undertook to recover the cotton and seed, her cargo, valued at £100,000, having been insured by underwriters of that port. When the wrecks of the *Zelda* and *Brinkburn*, which now lie side by side, were examined by divers in 1966, a number of iron cannon were found on the seabed between the two ships, indicating the site of a third and much older wreck. Another cannon site has recently been found on the western side of Maiden Bower, towards

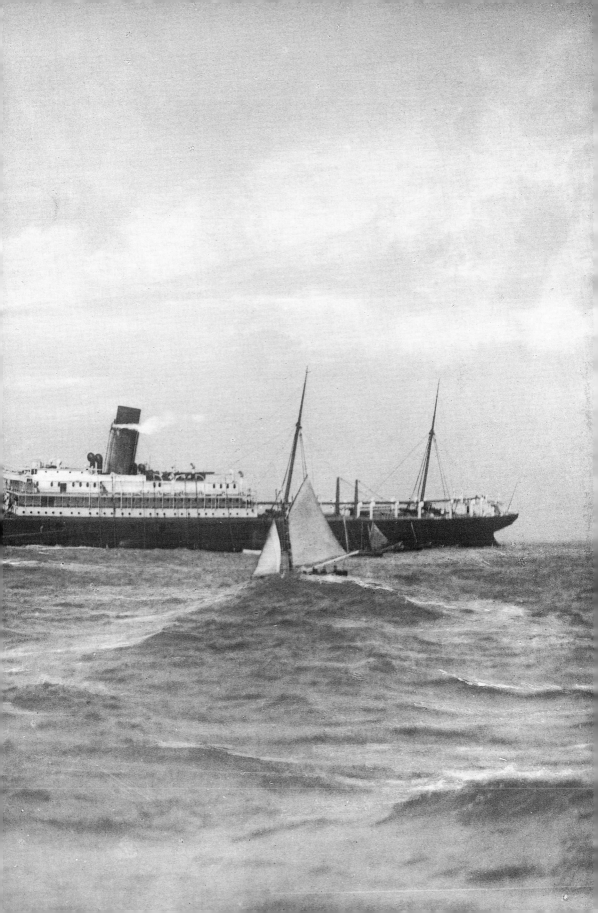

Maiden Bower Ledges.

Before continuing north to Scilly Rock, another notorious wreck area, some of the lesser-known incidents in the immediate vicinity are worth a mention. These include the Weymouth brig *Charming Molly*, Samuel Marder master, stranded and lost on Bryher on 20 November 1780 while carrying Portland stone to Dublin; the *Royal Standard*, a Kinsale brigantine, bound from her home port to Southampton with oats, which drove ashore on the morning of 11 January 1871, but was successfully refloated four days later. There was also the *Award* , a ship of 846 tons register owned in London but registered in Liverpool, which went ashore at Gweal in the early hours of 19 March 1861 while on her way to New Orleans in ballast. Her crew saved themselves by scrambling over the fallen foremast onto the rocks. Rough seas prevented any salvage work at the time, but she was later got off, only to go to pieces on the beach at Bryher on 28 March. Her fiddle-head and one quarter-board went to the Valhalla at Tresco; the other board served the New Inn, Tresco, as a sign for many years, and the salvage money paid for the wreck bought a new gig, the *Golden Eagle*, for the community.

Shipman Head, the northernmost point of Bryher, along with outlying Gweal and Scilly Rock, mark the extremities of a large indentation appropriately named Hell Bay. In winter or during severe north-west gales, Hell Bay is a fearful place and has the reputation of being a graveyard for ships. A West Indiaman, the *Queen Charlotte*, Jamaica-bound from Greenock under the command of Capt. Rayside, struck the Scilly Rock on 27 January 1815 and broke up. One seaman and three passengers lost their lives, the remaining thirteen clambering over the rocks and being stranded there for two days and nights before rescue. Two Bryher pilots, Charles Jackson and James Tregarthen, were drowned during their rescue, the latter having only recently returned home to Scilly after eight and a half years as a prisoner-of-war in French hands. The steamer *Egyptian Monarch* of London, 3,916 tons gross, New

York to London with a general cargo, cattle and some passengers, also struck here on 7 May 1888, but got off to reach Falmouth the same day with one compartment full of water. Less fortunate was the German full-rigged ship *Erik Rickmers* of Bremerhaven, which went ashore at 9.0 pm on 25 October 1899. This 2,050 tons gross vessel, built in 1897, was carrying rice from Bangkok for Bremen, and sank in deep water the same day that she went ashore.

When the Atlantic Transport Co's liner *Minnehaha* of 13,443 tons gross went aground on the eastern side of Scilly Rock at 12.50 am on 18 April 1910, there were islanders still living who clearly recalled another wreck by the same name on Peninnis Head, St Mary's, thirty-six years earlier, in 1874. On passage from New York to Tilbury with 171 crew, and sixty-six passengers all 1st class, the *Minnehaha* was also carrying general cargo and 243 steers. Capt. Sydney Leyland, the company's senior master mariner, had been unable to take an observation since the 14th of the month, and by noon on the 17th estimated that he was 170 miles from the Bishop and would pass at least six miles south of the lighthouse without any further changes of course. Fog dictated a reduction in speed to six knots during the evening, and although a sounding taken at midnight showed forty-seven fathoms, breakers were seen ahead only minutes later, and with scarcely more than a slight bump, the liner slid gently aground. Distress-guns fired by the Bishop light-keepers brought out the St Mary's lifeboat, but by the time it arrived at the wreck all the passengers had been landed by ship's boats on Bryher. The lifeboat stood by until 3 pm, when Capt. Leyland ordered everyone except his officers and a few members of the crew to board a waiting tug. The Falmouth tugs *Victor* and *Dragon*, summoned by urgent radio signals, arrived in time to see the crew start heaving cargo out of Nos 2 and 3 holds to lighten the ship, and throwing it into the sea. Brand-new motor-cars were winched outboard and dropped, followed by grand pianos, crated machinery of every description, sewing

machines, carpets and other valuable items by the ton. The frightened steers joined the rest of the cargo in the sea and, assisted by gigs whose crews roped the cattle alongside by their horns, at least 200 of the animals reached Bryher safely. A Lowestoft trawler came into St Mary's Roads with a crated motor-car on deck, having recovered it floating near the Wolf Rock. When asked what should be done with it, the Receiver of Wreck took the fishermen to the end of Hugh Town jetty and pointed out across the sound where dozens of similar crates could be seen bobbing about in the sea.

By the 20th, a fleet of tugs and salvage vessels were in attendance, and the serious business of getting the ship afloat again began. The first move on the part of the Liverpool Salvage Co and the Swedish firm which was assisting them, was to build a false floor of timber in each hold at low water, caulking each seam so as to make it watertight. Other false decks were built in succession at each hatch level, so that eventually six platforms were in position in each hold. The air compressors were then started but for days there was little

The Atlantic Transport Co's liner *Minnehaha* stranded on Scilly rock, 18 April 1910. After lightening ship by throwing overboard cars, pianos, sewing machines and 243 steers – all cargo, she was successfully refloated on 11 May and saved.

apparent result as the increasing pressure under the floors slowly pushed back the sea. Then on 11 May, while a group of British and Dutch divers were discussing some aspect of work on deck, they suddenly saw Bryher island begin to move across the horizon! Or rather, that was the impression the *Minnehaha* gave them as she refloated, much earlier than had been anticipated. Under her own power, she came off the ledges so fast that she nearly ran down the waiting tugs, whose assistance was not needed. Later, escorted by the tugs *Dragon*, *Triton* and *Victor*, plus the salvage vessels *Ranger*, *Belos*, *Linnet* and *Herakles*, the liner maintained a steady ten knots all the way to Falmouth, where she was anchored in St Just Pool and the remaining cargo discharged by local labour when the London stevedores specially brought to Cornwall went on strike. Registered and built at Belfast by Harland & Wolff in 1900, the

Minnehaha belonged to the same line that had owned the *Mohegan*, lost with 103 lives on the Manacles Rocks, Falmouth, in October 1898.

The final steamship wreck in this chapter, and perhaps the most dramatic, was that of the 6,827 tons gross Italian *Isabo* (ex-*Iris*), which went ashore during thick fog on the afternoon of 27 October 1927. There followed another of the island's dramatic rescues, comparable in its way with that of the *Delaware*. Ernest Jenkins, a Bryher coastguard, was the first man ashore to be aware of the wreck, having followed the sound of the *Isabo's* siren as she approached the islands. Shortly after, he heard the sound of escaping steam and voices. A telephone call at 5 pm to Matthew Lethbridge, coxswain of the St Mary's lifeboat *Elsie*, resulted in the boat being launched and heading for the north-west corner of Scilly in the record time of eight minutes. When the men of Bryher heard the news, they dropped everything and a mad scramble ensued as they manned the gigs kept at Great Par. Of the nineteen men who lived on the island, eighteen were at the scene of the wreck before the lifeboat! The nineteenth was missing because he had gone to another island, otherwise it would have been a full muster. The gig *Czar* was the first to reach the vicinity of Scilly Rock despite thick fog which reduced visibility to a few yards and a heavy swell that made rowing difficult. There the boat encountered a solid wall of floating wreckage: hatch covers, furniture, water tanks, mattresses, broken lifeboats, timber and wheat a foot thick on the surface. Then the heads and shoulders of men were seen above the debris, but so thick was the wreckage that the gig crews had difficulty in handling their oars, its only advantage being that it tended to flatten the sea somewhat. Eight men, almost naked, had been picked up by the *Czar* when the motor-boat *Ivy* arrived, but the floating grain soon choked her water circulating pump, and her engine was red hot by the time she had rescued one man. Meanwhile the *Czar* had picked up three more survivors and, grossly overloaded with nineteen on board, asked the *Ivy* to take eleven of them back to the island.

Another motor-boat, the *Sunbeam* from New Grimsby, arrived with a punt in tow, which proved to be the most useful craft in the rescue fleet. Manned by Charles and Edwin Jenkin, the small boat made three trips amongst the wreckage returning with a survivor on each occasion. With five of the steamer's crew safely on board, the *Sunbeam* then headed to seaward of the rocks where she found the *Isabo* ashore, broken in two just forward of the funnel. Groups of men clung to the stern section which was bumping badly, threatening to break off and sink at any moment. A line was passed across, and so eager were the crew to leave the wreck that there were as many as five men at one time on the rope. By the time the lifeboat from St Mary's arrived, men could still be seen in the rigging, but darkness, fog and heavily breaking seas around the wreck made it too dangerous for a close approach, and coxswain Lethbridge was obliged to take his boat to New Grimsby and anchor until daylight. As soon as it was sufficiently light, the lifeboat returned to find huge waves sweeping over the wreck, and only three men visible in the foremast rigging, while another, apparently dead, hung out of the crow's nest. Three rocket lines were fired; the first broke, the second fell short, the third fell squarely across its target only to lay untouched as the Italians appeared not to know what to do with it. Eventually, huge seas washed the three men from the wreck and they were picked out of the sea, the *Elsie* making three trips into dangerous water to reach them. Another survivor was sighted on Scilly Rock and a rocket line was fired across to him, but in reaching for the thin rope he was washed into the sea where he was picked up.

Of the *Isabo's* crew of thirty-eight, twenty-eight were saved, and in view of the appalling conditions under which the rescue was made, it was a feat as meritorious as any in the islands' long history. Before the survivors of the *Isabo* left the islands, they stood bareheaded on the jetty, with right arms extended in the Fascist salute while their captain, Alfredo Tarabocchia, said a prayer for the dead, and publicly thanked the men of Scilly who had saved their lives.

Stranded stern first in an inlet in Hell Bay, Bryher, the iron barque *Maipu*, wrecked in fog on 27 July 1879, in the process of being stripped of her steel yards and fittings, but she went to pieces before work was completed.

There was no shortage of recognition or thanks for the rescue, which showered in from all sides. The owners of the *Isabo* sent £70 to be shared amongst the lifeboat crew, and £250 for the people of Bryher who had taken the survivors in and given them clothing, with individual letters of thanks to all concerned. Matthew Lethbridge received two silver medals for his part, one from the Italian government, the other from the Royal National Lifeboat Institution. Charles Jenkins of the *Sunbeam* also received two silver medals, whilst Ernest Jenkins of the Ivy was awarded a silver medal from the Italian government and a bronze from the RNLI, as was W. E. Jenkins of the *Czar*. In addition, the Lifeboat Institution awarded four other bronze medals and twenty-one vellums, and the Italians a further thirty-four bronze medals. Registered at Lusinpicolo, the *Isabo* had been on passage from Montreal to Hamburg, and was supposedly thirteen miles south of the Bishop when she struck. Launched in January 1914 as the *Iris* by Cont. Nav.

Triestino, Montfalcone, she was fitted with an engine of 2,800 nhp built by the Glasgow firm of Rowan & Co.

The largest sailing ship wrecked in Hell Bay was the Liverpool barque *Maipu* of 594 tons gross. Bound from Iquique to Hamburg with a valuable cargo of saltpetre, she went ashore only a few hours prior to the *River Lune* which was wrecked in Muncoy Neck, St Agnes, also on 27 July 1879. With a crew of seventeen, the *Maipu* had called at Cork and was attempting to weather the Isles of Scilly in fog, when Capt. Thomas Wheeler thought he heard breakers ahead. The second mate went forward to listen, but could hear nothing for the sound of wind drumming in the foresail. Unsure of his position, the captain ordered the helm to be put up in order to wear ship but the order was never obeyed, for at that moment land was sighted ahead, under the lee bow. With helm hard down, spanker hauled taut and gaff topsails set, the *Maipu* started to come about, then struck the rocks a terrific blow and began to sink slowly by the bows. The *Maipu*, which had been launched at Birkenhead in 1865, was declared a total loss, and on 18 August, seventeen days after her wreck had been sold to some Bryher men for £7, she went to pieces on the beach.

East of Bryher, across the channel that constitutes New Grimsby harbour, lies Tresco, whose history is inextricably linked with the church, the sea and Augustus Smith in that order. Leyland, in his itinerary concerning the island of Tresco, wrote 'Iniscae longid to Tavestoke, and ther was a poore celle of Monkes of Tavestoke. Sum calle this Trescaw or St Nicholas Isle. In it ys a Iytle Pyle or fortres and a Paroch Chyrche that a Monke of Tavestoke yn peace doth serve as a membre to Tavestoke

Her stern underwater, the Liverpool barque *River Lune* lies a total wreck in Muncoy Neck, Annet, July 1879.

Abbey.' Tresco was the first island in Scilly to become 'civilised' following the establishment of the church, and after its dissolution during the Reformation, it became better known for its haven or anchorage, known as Old Grimsby. As trade increased and the size of ships calling at Scilly followed suit, Old Grimsby was found wanting and the deeper channel between Bryher and Tresco, known as New Grimsby, became the more popular anchorage. During the eighteenth and nineteenth centuries, Tresco enjoyed a lively interchange of shipping, and this small harbour would be crowded from end to end with sailing vessels.

Whilst Augustus Smith was not a Scillonian by birth, his interest and efforts were directed solely towards making something of the islands, to save them from the economic disaster which at the time seemed inevitable, and to bring them prosperity. It was in 1834 that he first took over the lease of the islands from the Duchy of Cornwall, leaving his property in Hertfordshire to live first on St Mary's, and then in a splendid house, known as the 'abbey' on Tresco, which has remained in the family

ever since. It was not without good cause that Augustus Smith earned several nicknames, including that of 'Emperor' Smith, for he was an autocrat of the old school, a hard, determined man, but far-sighted enough to see what the future could hold for Scilly. Some of his actions were very unpopular, such as forcing the inhabitants of the scattered and poverty-stricken off-islands to abandon their homes and settle in one of the five main communities. Having got the people together, he then introduced schools and, appreciating the long-term advantages of education, insisted that every boy be taught navigation. It paid off, and by 1860 there were 135 islanders holding master mariner's certificates. On his death in 1872, Augustus was succeeded by his nephew Lt Algernon Dorrien Smith, to whom the islanders owe the greatest debt, since it was he who introduced horticulture to the islands and built up the spring flower industry, now an essential part of the islands' economy. Algernon Dorrien-Smith—he later changed the order of his surnames—died in 1918, and was followed by Major Dorrien-Smith who survived until 1955, when the present member of the family, Lt-Cdr Dorrien-Smith, assumed some of the responsibilities of his forebears.

Hundreds of sailing ships entered and left both New and Old Grimsby every year, and as wrecks and strandings were all too common occurrences only a representative few can be mentioned here. One such was the ship *Nancy* which caught fire in New Grimsby on 9 March 1742. Carrying gunpowder, Bristol compound spirits, hemp and iron, she blew up and damaged several ships in the vicinity. Another was the brig *Oldenburger*, Hedstrum master, with a general cargo for Ostend from St Vincent, which dragged ashore and was wrecked on 24 January 1783. The *Governor Milne*, on passage from Grenada to London, parted her cables and went ashore on 10 January 1806, but was later got off and saved. A prize vessel, the *St Francis Apollo*, also went aground on 4 November 1806 and was refloated, as was the schooner *La Sidonia* on 10 September 1825, the *Delf* on 27 March 1831,

and the brigantine *Don*, of Sunderland, on 7 October 1846. At an unspecified location on Tresco, the *Mentor* of Jersey parted both her cables in a gale, drove athwart the French brig *Arthemise* and was cut down. The crew of the *Mentor* managed to get aboard the Frenchman, which was then run ashore on 18 February 1861 and became a total loss. Another brig, the *John & Ann* of London, was wrecked on 29 January 1826, but the French galliot *Maria*, which went ashore on 26 January 1812, was refloated on 14 March after repairs. A Norwegian barque from Fredrikstadt, the *Sophie*, which had been sold out of British service in 1888, started to disintegrate—presumably from old age—and was abandoned, together with her cargo of anthracite from Cardiff, on 14 December 1896. Towed later into New Grimsby by the *Lady of the Isles*, her hulk was sold to Algernon Dorrien Smith, who used her cargo to heat his greenhouses and her timbers around his estate on Tresco.

Elsewhere on Tresco, the Salcombe brig *Messenger*, laden with coal, Skentelbury master, dragged from the roadstead at St Mary's and went ashore on Skirt Island, to the south-west of Old Grimsby, on 28 October 1880. The St Mary's lifeboat, *Henry Dundas*, took off five men, and then stood by the wreck all night until daybreak as her captain and two men insisted on remaining with their ship. She was successfully refloated and saved on 30 October. A 2-ton cutter, locally owned and on its way to work the wreck of the steamer *Sussex*, capsized off Yellow Ledges on 30 December 1885 with the loss of one life.

Nut Rock was the scene of the sudden loss on 5 November 1801 of the London brig *Esperance*, carrying a cargo of locally-caught pilchards from Penzance to Venice. The *Esperance*, William Barber master, parted her anchor cables during a south-west gale, and within five hours of striking the rock the vessel had gone completely to pieces. A little to the north of Nut Rock lie the Paper Ledges, and it was here that the Italian barque *Rosa Tacchini* finished up after breaking adrift during a severe south-west gale on Friday, 22 November 1872.

On passage from Buenos Aires to Antwerp with hides, wool and tallow, she struck twice before settling on to the rocks, where she remained to become a total loss.

After striking Paper Ledge at the entrance to Tresco Flats, the Italian barque *Rosa Tacchini* was towed across to Carn Near on 22 November 1872, where she was broken up.

Opposite: Following a dive on the wreck of the Cypriot motor-vessel *Poleire,* in 1970, the author holds the builders name plate, found on the forward face of the bridge. She sank on Little Kettle Rock, Tresco, on 15 April 1970.

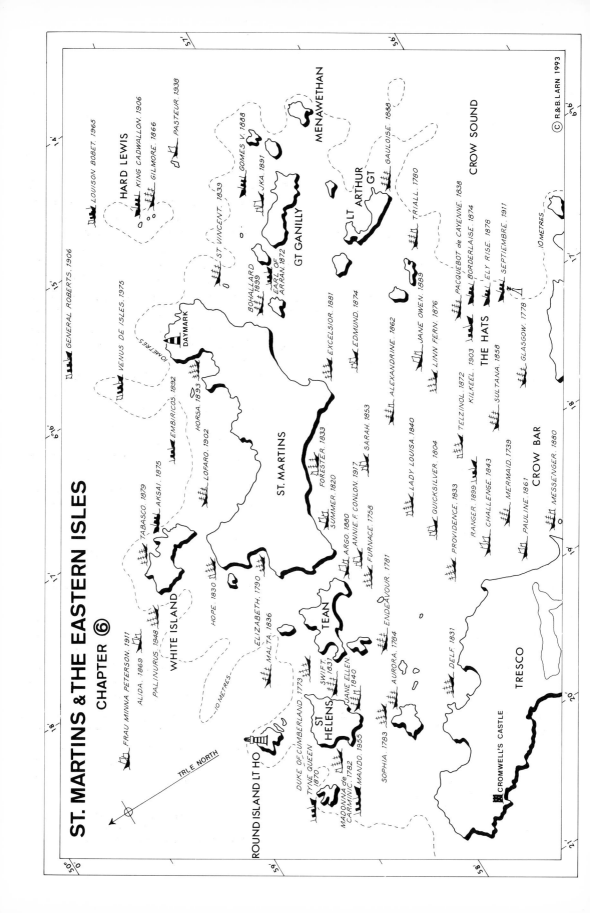

ST. MARTINS & THE EASTERN ISLES

CHAPTER 6

© R & B LARN 1993

CROW SOUND

MENAWETHAN

HARD LEWIS

GT GANILLY

GT ARTHUR

LT ARTHUR

ROUND ISLAND LT HO

TRI. E. NORTH

WHITE ISLAND

ST. MARTINS

DAYMARK

ST HELENS

TEAN

CROW BAR

THE HATS

TRESCO

CROMWELL'S CASTLE

LOUISON BOBET. 1965
KING CADWALLON. 1906
GILMORE. 1866
PASTEUR. 1938
GENERAL ROBERTS. 1906
VENUS DE ISLES. 1975
GOMES V. 1888
UKA. 1891
GAULOISE. 1888
ST. VINCENT. 1839
BOHALLARD. 1899
EARL OF ARRAN. 1872
TRIALL. 1780
FRAU MINNA PETERSON. 1911
ALIDA. 1869
PALINURUS. 1848
TABASCO. 1879
AKSAI. 1875
EMBIRICOS. 1892
LOFARO. 1902
HORSA. 1893
EXCELSIOR. 1881
EDMUND. 1874
ALEXANDRINE. 1862
JANE OWEN. 1883
LINN FERN. 1876
PACQUEBOT de CAYENNE. 1838
BORDERLAISE. 1874
ELY RISE. 1878
SEPTIEMBRE. 1911
FORESTER. 1833
SUMMER. 1820
SARAH. 1853
LADY LOUISA. 1840
QUICKSILVER. 1804
TELZINOL. 1872
KILKEEL. 1903
SULTANA. 1858
GLASGOW. 1778
HOPE 1830
ELIZABETH. 1790
MALTA. 1836
ARGO. 1880
ANNIE F. CONLON. 1917
FURNACE. 1758
PROVIDENCE. 1833
RANGER 1899
CHALLENGE. 1843
MERMAID. 1739
PAULINE 1861
MESSENGER. 1880
SWIFT. 1837
JANE ELLEN. 1840
ENDEAVOUR 1781
AURORA. 1784
DELF. 1831
DUKE OF CUMBERLAND. 1773
TYNE QUEEN. 1870
MADONNA de CARMINE. 1782
MANDO. 1955
SOPHIA. 1783

10 METRES

10 METRES

10 METRES

10 METRES

6

St Martins and the Eastern Isles

There is very little that can be said about St Martins or the Eastern Isles in modern times since their story lies deep in the past. Sprawled across the northern approaches to Scilly from Golden Ball to the easternmost tip of Menawethan, they present an almost continuous barrier of rock four miles long, aptly described as 'fringe islands'. Several islands bear the marks of some ancient habitation, with ruins and foundation stones of boundary walls reaching down to deserted foreshores. St Helens holds the remains of what is probably the oldest Christian building in the whole of Scilly; St Martins has several circular sepulchral barrows of some prehistoric race; whilst on Nornour, recent excavation has revealed what may be a metalsmith's workshop of Roman times complete with jewellery.

Apart from the *Torrey Canyon* which was wrecked on the Seven Stones reef, the last shipwreck of any size to occur at Scilly was that of the Panamanian steamship *Mando*, which went aground in fog on Golden Ball Bar at 8.30 pm on 21 January 1955. (See picture, p159.) Capt. Syras Svoronoss first radioed Lands End that his 7,176 tons gross ship. Hampton Roads for Rotterdam with 9,000 tons of coal, was in distress 120 miles west of the isles of Scilly. Several large vessels went to her assistance, including the MV *Cyprian Prince*, and the steamers *Greece Victory*, *Artillero* and *Vestfoss*, the latter already in the immediate vicinity but unable to locate the *Mando* in the dark. Lighthouse-keepers on the Round Island light first saw the Panamanian ship ashore, less than half a mile to their west, near Men-a-Vaur rocks, and summoned the St Mary's lifeboat.

Coxswain Matt Lethbridge, at the helm of the lifeboat *Cunard*, despite bad visibility and low water tidal conditions made the long journey around Samson, Bryher and Shipman Head in order to reach the distressed vessel,

but had no difficulty in locating her, the crew of the *Mando* having lit a bonfire of tar barrels on deck. Two of the motor-vessel's own boats had been lowered and filled with personal baggage by the time the lifeboat arrived, and at 11 pm, after persuading a somewhat reluctant captain to leave his ship, the *Cunard* headed back with the twenty-four crew aboard and two ship's boats in tow. The seventy-year-old gig *Sussex* arrived on the scene to assist in the rescue, and got within one hundred yards of the wreck before its crew realised that the *Mando* had already been abandoned. It would appear from existing records that the *Mando* was only the second vessel to be wrecked on Golden Ball Bar, the previous wreck having occurred 173 years earlier. This was the Venetian ship *Madonna de Carmine*, whose master had the splendid name of Basselle Vuclossaniach. Bound from Rotterdam to Smyrna with cloth, she was wrecked on 14 July 1782 and her crew had to sell part of her cargo in order to pay their passage to Falmouth.

Half-a-mile north-east of the bar, the lighthouse on Round Island nightly flashes out its ten-second red warning signal. The lighthouse was built by W.T. Douglass, concurrent with strengthening and raising the height of the Bishop light, and whereas, prior to its construction, Round Island had been a puffin colony, not a single puffin inhabited the island whilst the lighthouse remained manned. A Milford Haven-owned but Hull-registered steam trawler, the *General Roberts*, sank some distance offshore here on 5 June 1906. Almost ideal fishing conditions prevailed when the trawler reached the grounds some twelve miles north of St Martins at 8 pm that day, but before the

Overleaf: The bridge superstructure of the Liberian super-tanker *Torrey Canyon*, after the vessel broke in two, but before it was bombed and set on fire, 26 March 1967.

Heavy seas and successive storms soon caused the Panamanian registered Liberty ship *Mando* to break up, as she lay on the Golden Ball Bar after going ashore in dense fog on 21 January 1955.

trawl could be put out the engineer reported to Capt. John Pettit that they were making water. Pumps were started, but coal dust blocked the bilge-pump strainer boxes and in less than two minutes the vessel had settled low in the water. Her crew took to the punt and, riding to forty-five fathoms of log-line attached to the ship's rail, lay off to await events, until a freshening wind forced them to cast off and row for Round Island. For half an hour the masthead light of the *General Roberts* continued to burn, and was then extinguished as she foundered in forty fathoms.

Due to their proximity to Old Grimsby harbour on Tresco, St Helens Island, St Helens Pool and St Helens Gap have all been the site of several strandings. A snow from Boston, Mass, the *Duke of Cumberland*, carrying oil, lumber, deals and other timber for London, went ashore and was wrecked 25 September 1773. In the following year, on 1 February, the

Royd of London, bound from Barcelona to Roscoff with brandy and wine, parted her cables in a gale and was run onto a shoal. Capt. John London of the Teignmouth brig *Endeavour*, on passage from Liverpool to Portsmouth, also had to beach his vessel on 3 March 1781 in order to save life, but lost both his ship and her cargo of rum, brandy, coal and herrings. Ashore on 27 March 1831, the same day that the *Delf* went onto the rocks in Old Grimsby harbour, the *Swift*, Bond master, Liverpool to Rotterdam, grounded on St Helens while proceeding to sea but got off on the next tide, a happier fate than that of the Beaumaris brig *Jane Ellen*, Bangor to London with slate, wrecked on St Helens on 17 March 1840. Other minor incidents concerned the *Sophia* of London, Viborg to Liverpool with deals, which stranded and sank 25 November 1783, and the *Aurora*, Robert Dixon master, which struck a rock off Land's End but managed to reach St Helens Gap before sinking on 31 December 1784. She was later salvaged and returned to service. There was also the *Malta*, Cardiff to Malta with coal, wrecked on Black Rock, seaward of St Helens Gap, on 29

December 1835; and the steamer *Tyne Queen* of Liverpool, Cardiff to Marseilles, which struck Men-a-Vaur in fog at 8 am on 21 July 1870 and was on the rocks in St Helens Pool for an hour before reaching New Grimsby and discharging her cargo.

Between St Helens and St Martins lies the islet of Tean where, in 1852, a wooden box marked 'Agnes Ewing' was washed ashore. It was later identified as having come from an East Indiaman of that name on passage from Liverpool to Calcutta, but nothing more was ever heard of either ship or crew. In 1880, the 61-ton wooden schooner *Argo* went ashore on Tean Island, and was so badly damaged that she became a total wreck. Owned by John Small of Bridgwater but registered at Dublin, the *Argo* had left Newport on 22 October with 105 tons of anthracite for Polruan, Fowey. At midnight, when about twenty miles west of Lundy, she shipped a heavy sea which split her mainsail, carried away both gangways and broke her boat gripes. It was only by chance that her master, going below to collect a towel, found two feet of water in the cabin. Her pumps were promptly manned, and the *Argo* bore away for Scilly with frequent seas breaking clean over her. At 7 pm lights were sighted ahead, but in making towards them the *Argo* struck a ledge, and, despite having both anchors down, dragged ashore on 23 October. Her crew of eight took to the rigging, awaiting low tide and daybreak, when they were able to gain the shore without incident. Only four days later, on 28 October, the 194 tons gross wooden brig *Messenger* of Salcombe dragged onto Skirt Island but was refloated after the St Mary's lifeboat had saved five of her crew. Carrying steam coal from Cardiff to Portsmouth, and owned by Abraham Skentelberry of Looe, the brig, which had been launched in 1866 by Gough of Bridgwater, was so badly damaged that she had to be broken up.

Of the many wrecks on St Martins, the largest of the 'fringe islands', the earliest authenticated occurred on 20 April 1790. This was the *Elizabeth* of London, laden with salt from Alicante, which was sighted coming up on

the evening tide, her mainmast overboard, decks smashed and a tangle of rigging trailing astern. Every effort was made to get her ashore, but she drifted right round the Scillies three times before finally beaching itself on St Martins. Some forty years later the brig *Hope* was homeward bound from Africa to London with a valuable cargo when, on 19 January 1830, her master, Alfred Noble, mistook the St Martins daymark for the St Agnes lighthouse during fog, got too close inshore and struck a rock on the north side of the island. Of the two boats which got away from the wreck, one contained a Dutch naval officer and his wife, a negro servant and another passenger, all of whom were killed or drowned when the vessel's mainmast collapsed across their boat, smashing it to pieces; the other boat with Capt. Noble, the mate and four of the crew on board, reached shore safely. One hundred casks of palm oil, 300 elephant tusks, a box of silver dollars and two small boxes of gold dust valued at £400 each were salvaged. St Martins daymark, a prominent, 20-ft high conical tower erected in the 1680s by Thomas Ekins, a steward of the islands, had until then been plastered white, but after the tragic loss of the *Hope* it was repainted red, and later with the red and white horizontal stripes it bears today.

On 13 February 1833, the naval brig-sloop *Forester*, a 'Cherokee' class vessel of 10 guns and 229 tons (bm), launched at Chatham dockyard on 28 August 1832, struck the Crow Ledge and drifted ashore onto some rocks near St Martins. On passage from Plymouth to Africa, she was got off on the 26th and towed back to the naval base by the steamer *Rhadamano*. A number of iron cannon lie on the seabed to the south of Menawethan, and it has been suggested these were the guns from the *Forester*, thrown overboard to lighten ship. A French chassemarée, the *St Vincent*,

Overleaf: After stranding in Bread and Cheese cove, St Martin's, on 4 April 1893, the full-rigged ship *Horsa* was found to be leaking badly from torn plates. Escorted by the packet steamer *Lyonesse*, the *Horsa* attempted to sail herself round Scilly and get into St Mary's Road, but filled and sank 21 miles south-west of the Bishop Rock.

commanded by Capt. Ris, struck and sank on 6 December 1839 near the Chimney Rocks, to the eastern end of St Martins, but all her crew were saved and three-quarters of her cargo of barley from Marans, intended for Penzance, was salvaged before she went to pieces.

Sunday morning, 27 November 1881, saw the 640 tons register, iron barque *Excelsior* of Hamburg at anchor in St Mary's Roads in bad weather. Despite a hundred fathoms of cable out on the port anchor, eighty on the starboard and stoppers to ease the strain on the windlass, both cables parted, and at 3 pm she drove towards Crow Bar. The St Mary's lifeboat and two gigs put out in answer to her distress signals, but though on board her crew were frantically cutting down her topmasts and slipping the broken cables, they could not prevent the five-year old, German-built barque from striking the bar, and finally Cruthers Point at the south-western corner of Higher Town Bay. There she lay on the rocks for the best part of two months until 22 January 1882 when, at the top of high water, with the 64-ton *Queen of the Bay* lashed alongside and the *Lady of the Isles* in the lead, the tow towards St Mary's began. Despite two steam pumps on her deck, both working full bore, it was obvious within fifteen minutes of the tow starting that the men were fighting a losing battle. Half an hour later the barque heeled over to port and sank, taking the valuable steam pumps with her, as well as breaking off the *Queen of the Bay's* mainmast and damaging her bridge, railings and paddle-boxes. The *Excelsior* had left Rangoon on 7 June, Rudolf Loose master, with a crew of fifteen and 915 tons of rice, rattan and teak, and had been bound for Scilly for orders.

Whilst no steamers have been lost on St Martins itself, several have hit outlying rocks such as White Island, Hard Lewis or the Hats, the Greek ship *Embiricos* being a typical example. Heavy rain, which seriously reduced visibility during the early hours of Saturday, 6 February 1892, caused the steamer to strike a rock at the back of St Martins, probably either John Thomas or Deep Ledge. So thick was the weather that her lookouts caught a brief glimpse of Round Island light only seconds before breakers were seen and she struck. Capt. J. Lukisias ordered the ship to be abandoned by her crew of twenty-five and the starboard-side boat, manned by twelve crew plus three Maltese seamen who were passengers on board, was successfully lowered. Within fifteen minutes, the *Embiricos* of Andros, a ship of 1,256 tons register, went down by the stern, foundering in forty fathoms. She took with her the captain, mate bo'sun and three others who were attempting to launch the port-side boat. Twenty-eight hours later four of her crew—three engineers and one seaman—were rescued from a boat found off the Lizard by the British steamer *Rutland* and landed at Le Havre. The *Embiricos*, built in 1889 by Mcilwaine & McCall of Belfast, owned by A. Embiricos of Andros, and valued at £20,000, had left Cardiff with coal for Malta and Odessa only the previous afternoon.

Although the full-rigged sailing ship *Horsa* of Liverpool finally sank twenty-one miles south-west of the Bishop Rock on Tuesday, 4 April 1893, it was the rocks in Bread and Cheese Cove, St Martins which tore the holes in her plating. (Picture, p 17.) Homeward bound under Capt. Rolson, from Bluff Harbour, New Zealand with tinned meat, wool and grain, this 1,163 tons gross, iron ship came too close inshore while weathering St Martins during a full easterly gale, missed stays and went hard aground. The St Mary's lifeboat was called out and arrived to find the *Horsa* settling down on the ebb tide. That same afternoon, on the flood, after Mrs Rolson, her child and nurse had landed, the packet steamer *Lyonesse* went alongside, passed a tow rope and pulled the *Horsa* off. During the tow, which went on well into the evening, three ropes were broken and eventually Capt. Rolson decided to sail his ship the rest of the way to St Mary's, but asked the packet to remain in attendance. It was fortunate that he did, for she was able to rescue his entire crew when the *Horsa* rolled over and sank at 1.30 in the morning. Owned by the Star Navigation Co of Liverpool, the *Horsa* had been launched by Scotts of Greenock in 1860.

During a full south-westerly gale on 16 February 1869, the Dutch schooner *Alida* of Veendam, Swansea to Taragonna with patent fuel, was lost off White Island while attempting to reach St Mary's with a bad leak. Her crew were rescued by the pilot-gig *Linnet* just as she was about to sink. Another steamer lost in the same area was the Russian *Aksai*, early in the morning of 2 November 1875. She was on passage from Cardiff to Odessa with coal, and when fog blurred the outline of the Scillies Capt. Boltine took her along the north side of St Martins, only to strike White Island and remain fast. Again, it was the *Lady of the Isles* which went to the rescue of her captain and crew of thirty-nine, leaving the steamer to go to pieces where she lay. A 215-ton Bordeaux barquentine, the *Tabasco*, with 300 tons of coal and bottled beer valued at £150 from Greenock, also struck and sank on White Island on 24 March 1879. Her loss was attributed to a language barrier between the English and French members of the crew, and to her master having mistaken the Seven Stones lightship for Trevose Head. The *Tabasco* was, in fact, only two weeks off the stocks, and on her maiden voyage.

Distress rockets and flares normally herald a wreck, but it was the bellowing of frightened cattle on shore that first gave the alarm to the islanders of St Martins on 27 December 1848 when the ship *Palinurus*, Gorl master, Demerera to London, went ashore on the Lion Rock during a north-east gale. It was the noise made by the wind in her torn and thrashing sails that had alarmed the grazing animals. All seventeen of her crew drowned, twelve of the bodies coming ashore on St Martins on 5 January, and two more on the l9 January. Nine quarter casks of rum, plus seventy-one puncheons and fourteen hogsheads of spirit were saved by the islanders.

Another large sailing ship in trouble nearby was the Neapolitan barque *Lofaro*, Hamburg to Cardiff in ballast, which struck the Merrick Rock, close to White Island on 2 February 1902. A St Martins coastguard was the first to see the vessel, but did not notice anything

Possibly the only Russian steamship ever lost amongst the Isles of Scilly, the coal laden *Aksai* was wrecked at the back of St Martin's, on White Island, 2 November 1875.

Fog, the prime cause of so many wrecks around Scilly, resulted in the Glasgow registered *King Cadwallon* stranding on the Hard Lewis rocks on 22 July 1906, where she became a total loss.

amiss and had left the watch-house to have his tea by the time the ship was close inshore. Lighthouse-keepers on Round Island fired the distress rockets which summoned the St Mary's lifeboat, while fourteen local men manned the gig *Emperor*, only to be beaten back by high seas as they attempted to round St Martins Head. From the shore, anxious watchers saw men swimming away from the wreck, but by dark none of them had come ashore. By the time the lifeboat arrived it was quite dark, so dark in fact that the coxswain had to call to those ashore in order to establish his position from time to time. They searched around the Devil's Table with lanterns but found only wreckage, and were then forced to make the perilous return journey along the north side of St Martins, past

Round Island and through Tean Sound. Next morning the wrecked vessel's keel, complete with stem and stern post, was found ashore, along with three bodies and a wooden chest. Ship's papers and a captain's gold watch in the chest identified the wreck as the 664-ton *Lofaro*, launched at Savona in 1876, which had left Hamburg on 14 January.

Half-a-mile off-shore from St Martins Head, the Hard Lewis Rocks thrust up from 200 feet of water, rocks that have taken the bottom out of at least two ships, and probably others. It has been claimed and generally accepted that a barque called the *Chieftain* was wrecked on Hard Lewis in 1856, and a figurehead of a Highland chieftain in full-dress in the Valhalla, plus a piece of ship's timbers in a Penzance restaurant, are offered as evidence, but in fact there was no such wreck. No doubt the figurehead was washed in from some wreck offshore, perhaps a ship with a Scottish name or connection, but the records of Lloyd's, the Board of

A French crabber registered at Cameret, the *Pasteur*, stranded on Hanjague 12 September 1938.

Trade, Royal National Lifeboat Institution and the Customs and Excise show no *Chieftain* as being afloat at or about that time.

A wreck on the Hard Lewis which can, however, be substantiated was that of the 535 tons net barque *Gilmore* of Southampton, Duff master, on 12 April 1866. She was on her way to Quebec from Southampton in ballast when she struck, and her crew got away in their own boats just as she foundered. Fog, the prime cause of so many losses around Scilly. put the 2,126 tons net King Line steamer *King Cadwallon* of Glasgow ashore on the same rocks at 5 am on 22 July 1906. After loading 5,032 tons of coal at Barry, shipped by the Tredeager Coal & Iron Co of Cardiff, Capt. George Mowat and his crew of twenty-six had sailed at 8 am on 21 July, bound for Naples. The *King Cadwallon* left harbour in dense fog which continued until they were off Lundy, when it thinned for half-an-hour, long enough for the captain to obtain an accurate position fix. From

Lundy, the steamer was set on a course of s56°w until the log showed a distance of seventy-seven miles had been covered, when the heading was altered to s34°w. Dense fog prevailed throughout the passage, but frequent soundings showed no sign of shoaling water. At 4.57 am a sounding showed twenty-seven fathoms (162 ft), yet three minutes later she struck rocks, listed to starboard, and within ten minutes the forehold was completely flooded. Later, she slipped back into deep water and foundered, to lie close to the wreck which has been claimed to be that of the *Chieftain* but is almost certainly that of the *Gilmore*. Close at hand, Hanjague Rock made a backdrop for the spectacular stranding of the French crabber *Pasteur* of Cameret on 12 September 1938. She was leaving Scilly when the wind dropped and she drifted ashore, fortunately to be refloated

An early Penzance/Scillies packet, the paddle-steamer *Earl of Arran*, was lost on Irishman's Ledge, Nornour, when her captain listened to the advice of an island passenger, and took a so called 'short-cut' to reach St Mary's, 16 July 1872.

on the next high tide.

In 1872, island communications suffered a double catastrophe in the loss of both packet steamers, the *Little Western* being wrecked on Southward Well on 6 October, and the auxiliary packet *Earl of Arran*, a Clyde-built paddle-steamer, grounding on Irishman's Ledge on 16 July. The *Earl of Arran* left Penzance about 10 am bound for St Mary's with a crew of eight hands, 100 passengers, mail and some general cargo. On reaching the islands Captain Richard Deason gave the excursionists the opportunity to see something of the Eastern Isles by allowing Stephen Woodcock, a Scillonian hobbler, to take the vessel between St Martin's Head and Hanjaque, thereby it seems, saving 20 mins. Woodcock put the steamer too close to the rocks and she struck heavily on Irishman's Ledge. Her engine was put full-astern, but she struck again and again. Her boats were then lowered, and all the ladies

taken off first; the vessel then being run ashore on Nornour. By 3pm all the passengers, luggage, fittings and some stores had been saved, by now her engine-room and lower areas having flooded. Two days later she broke in two, the owners receiving only £1,000 in compensation, despite the fact she had cost them £3,000. Her engine was recovered by the Western Marine Salvage Co, but her boiler still shows at low water. The passengers and the whole of the cargo were saved, but nothing could be done for the paddle-steamer and she was broken up for scrap after she broke in two. At a Board of Trade enquiry Captain Deason was found guilty of a grave error in allowing a passenger, of whose competency he had no knowledge, to take charge of his ship, and his certificate was suspended for four months. Built at Paisley in 1860 for the Ardrossan to Arran passenger run, the *Earl of Arran* served on the Clyde from 1860 until 1868, when she worked excursions between Ayr and Troon before going south to Scilly in 1869. (Picture, p 169.)

The Padstow schooner *J.K.A.*, Escott master, Ballinacurra to Poole with 86 tons of oats, was wrecked on the Shag Rocks, near the Mouls, on 11 November 1891. Owned by William Escott of Watchet, the 60-ton schooner's passage had been uneventful until 5 am on the day she was wrecked. When close to Scilly, the *J.K.A.* encountered a moderate SSE gale, which quickly swung round to the NNW and increased in force, throwing the vessel on her beam ends. All her canvas was taken in and when the vessel was brought before the wind and righted it was discovered that her port bulwarks and everything movable on deck had been washed away. Her mainboom then fell down over the starboard quarter, carrying away the rail and bulwarks, preventing the wheel from being turned. She drifted helpless until 6.45 am when land was sighted, which at first was not recognised. When close inshore both anchors were dropped, but the cables soon parted and she drove onto the rocks. Her crew abandoned ship and reached Great Innisvouls, from where they were rescued by a St Martins gig, by which time the schooner had drifted clear and foundered. Another of the smaller

wrecks in the same area was the 76-ton, wooden brigantine *Bohallard* of Nantes, lost near English Island on 12 February 1899. Bound from Newport to Audierne with coal, the *Bohallard* parted her cables in St Mary's Roads during a WNW hurricane and went ashore at Pendrathen. Later, she floated clear, only to be lost in Higher Town Bay, near the Carn, when she broke up on the 14th.

When St Martins pilots found nineteen members of a steamer's crew and one passenger drifting seaward past Hanjague on 9 August 1888 in two ship's boats, it was the first that anyone knew of the foundering of the Portuguese steamer *Gomes V.* Under Capt. Antonio d'Azevedo, the vessel had sailed from Cardiff the previous day, loaded with 629 tons of steam coal consigned to H. Kendall of Oporto. At 1.30 am on the 9th dense fog had

As a direct result of losing his Penzance/St Mary's steam packed, the *Little Western*, on Southward Well on 6 October 1872, Captain Hicks was banished from the Isles of Scilly.

been encountered and, despite her speed having been reduced to dead slow, she struck the Shag Rock before the lookouts even saw land ahead. Distress rockets were fired and the crew took to the boats, but fortunately they were sighted before they had time to drift out to sea. At high water, the wreck lay completely submerged and it took until 18 October for divers to recover all that was required, mostly steam winches, anchor cables and deck fittings. A comparatively new ship, the 736 tons gross *Gomes V*, of Lisbon, owned by Alonco Gomes, had been launched as the *Strathcarron* in 1883 by Bursell & Sons of Dumbarton.

That same year, Great Arthur Island, on the northern edge of Crow Sound, claimed the 332-ton barque *Gauloise* of Bordeaux, Raul Herand master, at 3 am on 15 January. With a crew of eleven, she was carrying 437 tons of pit-props to Porthcawl and was under plain sail heading NNE, with St Agnes light visible about fourteen miles ahead, when fog came down. Despite a good lookout, nothing was seen until 2.10 am when the mate went aloft to the fore-yard and saw rocks all round them. He ordered the helmsman to luff-up, but when the master countermanded the order, the vessel missed stays and fell away. Despite her main and fore-yards being backed, she drove onto Great Arthur. Her crew took to the boats, but later re-embarked to find that the ship's hull had been pierced by a large rock. Her cargo was worked out at intervals during the following six months, after which what little remained and the hulk itself were sold for £14 10s to Joseph Delley of Penzance, who burnt her to the waterline to get at the remaining timber.

Approaching the Isles of Scilly from the east, unless one is familiar with the islands, the wide expanse of Crow Sound can be deceptive. At first glance it would appear to be a wide, deep sound, flanked only by St Mary's to the south and Great Arthur and the Gannicks to the north, whereas, in fact, it is the most dangerous of the main approaches to St Mary's Roads, as many a ship's master has found to his cost. Untold numbers of incidents have occurred in the Sound, or else on the Hats Ledges and

Crow Bar which straddle the channel, though fortunately most have been cases of vessels going aground and being subsequently refloated. On 31 August 1780, the brig *Tryal* of Bristol, laden with sugar and cotton from St Christopher, was wrecked in Crow Sound, and a French barque bound from Rio de Janeiro to Havre, the *Pacquebot de Cayenne*, C.T. Muny master, drove onto the Hats during a full SSE gale on 27 November 1838 and was lost. Although her crew were saved, when the vessel bilged and broke up most of her cargo of hides, wool and coffee was washed out. It was said that she also carried a large sum of money in silver dollars.

Four steamers have fallen victim to the Hats, two of which left their rusting plates scattered over the sand, the first of the quartet being the 379 tons net *Bordelaise* of Liverpool, bound from Newport to Oporto with coal and railway iron. On 4 April 1874, Capt. O'Keefe attempted to bring his vessel in at half-tide without a pilot on board, and was about to anchor when she struck heavily. Anxious to save their vessel which had been built at Whiteinch only the previous year, the owners, the Boscawen Steamship Co of Liverpool, ordered out lighters to remove the cargo and had special salvage pumps brought down from Glasgow. But shortly after the pumps had been installed on deck, the *Bordelaise* sank, and divers had to be employed to salvage the equip-ment. After almost all the cargo had been saved, the hull and engines were sold to Francis Banfield & Sons for £455. The *Ely Rise* of Cardiff was the next steamship incident on the Hats. While attempting to gain the shelter of St Mary's Roads during a westerly gale on Wednesday, 23 October 1878, Capt. William Vickerman took his ship into Crow Sound at 5.30 pm with the tide at half-ebb, and struck the rocks. Within an hour her engine-room was flooded and the boiler fires extinguished. Hand-pumps were rigged and, with the *Lady of the Isles* alongside, the *Ely Rise* was kedged off and beached for repairs, afterwards going alongside St Mary's jetty. Bad weather brought the Spanish steamer *Setiembre* into the Sound on Sunday, 26 March 1911. Registered at Bilbao, and bound from Porman to Maryport with iron-ore, this 2,171 tons net vessel lost her rudder and badly holed her hull when she hit the Hats. By midnight, she had flooded from end to end and although her entire cargo of ore was dumped overboard in an attempt to lighten her, she was eventually abandoned to the sea. Her boiler still shows above the surface at low water, a point of interest to holiday-makers visiting the eastern isles in local launches. Fourth and last victim was the *Kilkeel*, Glasgow to Nova Scotia with a general cargo, which struck the Hats on entering Crow Sound with choked pumps on 17 October 1903 but was successfully refloated later.

That wide expanse of shallow water north of the Hats, known as St Martins Flats, saw the 95-ton Brixham schooner *Sarah* sink at anchor on 27 January 1853. Bound from Cardiff to Tenerife and Santa Cruz with a crew of six and a cargo of coal, she sprang a serious leak on the 25th and had to be brought into the Sound.

Her hull and cargo were sold three weeks later for £38. A Cardiff brig, the *Alexandrina*, laden with coal, was abandoned in the roadstead on 24 February 1862 during a gale, but pilots saved her by running the vessel on to the flats, a service for which they received £97 from a grateful owner. The schooner *Edmund* was involved in a similar incident on 13 April 1874.

At low tide, the worst obstacle in the Sound is Crow Bar and the ledges around Guthers Island, which have been the cause of innumerable strandings and incidents over the centuries. On 30 December 1739, the *Mermaid* of Plymouth was wrecked on the bar, and on 20 January 1758 the *Furnace* of London on Broad Ledge, after striking Guthers. Bound for Gosport, William Park master, the *Furnace* was carrying brandy, pewter, oil, rosin and prunes,

Having lost her rudder, the Spanish steamship *Setiembre* entered Crow Sound on 26 March 1911, but struck and sank on the Hats. Despite dumping her entire cargo of iron-ore overboard, she would not refloat, and became a total loss.

and although she sank, Customs officers and local inhabitants saved most of her cargo. HMS *Glasgow*, a 20-gun, 6th rate struck the Crow in 1778 and exchanged part of her forefoot for a huge rock which she carried back to Plymouth embedded in her hull. Launched by Blaydes of Hull on 31 August 1757, the *Glasgow* was lost by fire in Montego Bay, Jamaica, the following year. Other incidents here involved the *Quicksilver*, carrying a cargo of salt for Newfoundland and totally wrecked on 30 May 1804; the schooner *Summer*, run on shore on

The remains of the Norwegian barque *Sophie* lying on Tresco beach near New Grimsby. Towed in derelict and full of anthracite on 14 December 1896. Note that her hawse pipes have been enlarged into windows, suggesting someone made the wreck their home on the beach.

28 November 1808; the *Providence*, bound for Bombay, which struck on 13 February 1833, was scuttled two days later, then raised and floated off on 6 May; and the less fortunate *Lady Louisa*. This was a brig owned in London, Henley master, which arrived at Scilly in distress whilst bound from Rio de Janeiro to Cowes and London with coffee on 2 February 1840. Unfavourable weather and tidal conditions made it impossible to get her to the anchorage, and she drove onto Guthers Bar. Hundreds of bags of cargo were thrown overboard, but she remained fast and eventually went to pieces.

On 21 November 1843, the London schooner *Challenger*, Surinam to her home port, struck the Nundeeps and sank near Bryher island, and a German ship, the *Sultana*

of Hamburg, was totally wrecked there on 24 March 1853. Her crew were all drowned, and a nameboard from the wreck was washed ashore as far afield as Padstow nearly a month later. Other casualties on Crow Bar have included the *Pauline,* a French schooner bound from Ardrossan to Rouen with railway iron, which drove ashore on 18 February 1861 and went to pieces; *Telxinoi,* a Greek brig, on 17 February 1872; a full-rigged ship from Glasgow, the *Linn Fern,* totally wrecked on 9 March 1876, and the *Jane Owen,* another total loss on 3 March 1889. The Liverpool Salvage Association's steamer *Ranger* also struck the bar on 7 June 1899, but was refloated the same day.

The navigational chart for the Isles of Scilly shows a wreck situated 100 yards north-west of Broad Ledge, at the entrance to Tean Sound. This is the American schooner *Annie F. Conlon,* which was badly damaged by gunfire from a German submarine, and was towed into Crow Sound on 5 October 1917. She began to break up immediately on arrival, and her cargo, consisting of casks of oil, washed clear. By 1 December she was a complete wreck, masts and deck gone, her hull lying on its beam ends, and empty of all cargo. A total of 455 casks of oil were salvaged and realised £1,406 9s for the owners, the Marine Transport Co of Mobile, Alabama.

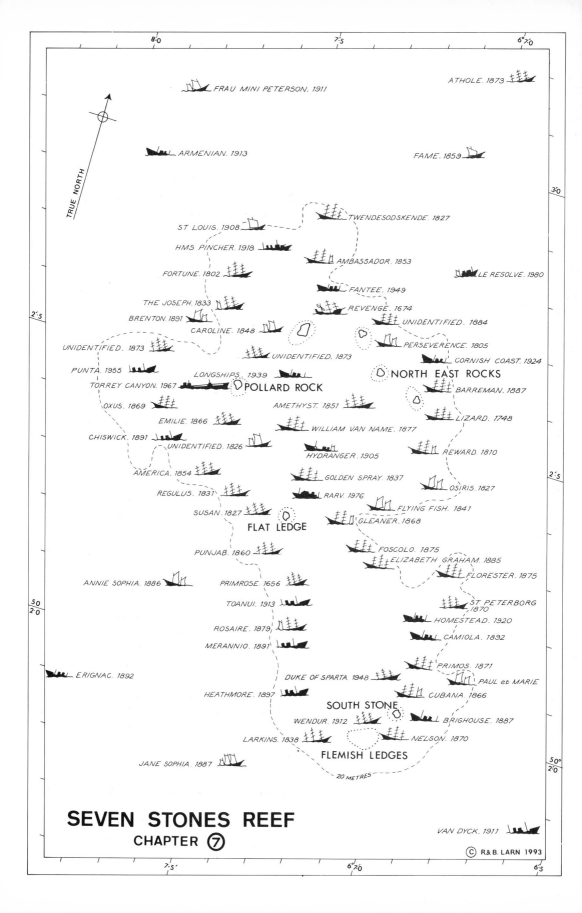

SEVEN STONES REEF

CHAPTER ⑦

7

The Seven Stones

Until 1967 the quiet notoriety enjoyed by the Seven Stones Reef was understandable, since its infamous reputation for wrecks concerned only the Cornish and seafarers. Then on Saturday 18 March, a ship whose name was to become familiar to half the world went ashore on the reef to give the West Country and the British government a problem of unprecedented magnitude. Besides being the largest ship ever lost by stranding on the coast of the United Kingdom, the *Torrey Canyon* was, at the time, one of the largest tankers in the world and was carrying a prodigious 119,328 tons of crude oil when she hit the Pollard Rock, tearing a 610-ft-long gash in her starboard side. Since 1967, there have been at least 85 vessels larger than the *Torrey Canyon* lost at sea, several of which were tankers, resulting in massive oil spills. The nearest of these to the United Kingdom was the Liberian registered *Amoco Cadiz*, 109,700 tons gross, which was wrecked on 16 March 1978 near Ushant. She broke in two the following day, depositing 223,000 tonnes of crude oil on the coast, giving the French authorities no time to contain the spill.

A radio message from the *Torrey Canyon*, sent at 8.45 am to the agent in Milford Haven, stated simply: 'Aground on Seven Stones. Require immediate assistance.' It was one of the nearby fishing trawlers, probably the French *Mater Christi*, that informed the world on an international distress frequency of the stranding, and so swung the rescue organisation into action. The St Mary's lifeboat was launched, two 'search and rescue' helicopters lifted off from the naval air station at Culdrose, and several ships reported that they were closing the wreck at full speed. These included the Fleet Auxiliary *Brambleleaf*, only thirteen miles south of the 'Stones', the Dutch motor-vessel *Bierum*, the British tanker *Tillerman*, the steamship *Helenus*, and the tugs *Atlantic*,

Albatross and *Utrecht*. The latter, a huge, Dutch, ocean-going, salvage vessel, was on her regular station in Mounts Bay, and reached the Seven Stones shortly after the lifeboat.

The deck watch aboard Trinity House lightship No 19, the Seven Stones lightship, first saw the huge vessel at 9.05 am, three or four miles from their position, thus putting the tanker between three-quarters and a mile and three-quarters south of the Pollard Rock. Warning rockets were fired, followed by the international flag hoist 'JD' meaning, 'You are standing into danger', the same signal being flashed repeatedly on a lamp. Assuming that the time of the stranding given by the captain of the tanker was correct, then the crew of the Seven Stones lightship were attempting to warn the *Torrey Canyon* of danger after she had in fact gone ashore. The time factor is still in dispute but is irrelevant, since the lightship had no operative responsibility to warn individual ships, its mere presence being considered sufficient. That such a disaster could happen in broad daylight, with near perfect visibility and a relatively calm sea, within easy visual range of the Wolf Rock lighthouse, Round Island light, the Longships and the Seven Stones lightship itself is almost inconceivable; but happen it did and the monstrous vessel finally impaled itself at seventeen knots on the biggest and western-most rock of the reef.

By 11 am, a small fleet had gathered off the reef, maintaining a respectful distance between themselves and the broken water which marked the rocks. Situated fifteen miles west of Lands End and seven miles from the Isles of Scilly, the reef is supposedly named after seven rocks, whereas in fact there are eight, which protrude above the surface at low water, the whole occupying an area of some three-quarters of a square mile. As the tide fell and more broken water appeared around the stranded vessel, only the lifeboat was able to go alongside her, and to transfer salvage officers and other experts. After one such trip, coxswain Matt Lethbridge of the St Mary's *Guy and Clare Hunter,* expressed a fear that the wreck would soon break its back. Eight and a half days later his prophecy came true, but only after the *Torrey Canyon* had survived three attempts to refloat her, two gales, and an internal explosion. By the afternoon of her first day ashore, an estimated 5,000 tons of the dark brown oil had spilled from her ruptured tanks, and already pollution was on a scale never previously experienced. Devonport dockyard despatched the minesweeper HMS *Clarbeston* with 1,000 gallons of detergent to emulsify and sink the oil, followed by the tug *Sea Giant* with a further 3,500 gallons, almost the entire stock held by the Royal Navy. The *Utrecht* made the first attempt to refloat the tanker alone that evening at high water, but failed to move her, after which the weather deteriorated so that by morning a full gale was blowing from the northwest. Aircraft were already reporting an oil slick covering an area of eighteen miles by two, spreading into the English Channel and towards Cornwall. HMS *Barrosa*, already in attendance off the Seven Stones, joined the *Clarbeston* in spraying detergent, but it was already painfully obvious that their efforts were totally inadequate to even keep pace with the flood of oil. During the early hours of Sunday afternoon the *Torrey Canyon* was abandoned by all except her captain, her principal officers, four of the crew and two salvage experts. The St Mary's lifeboat, relieved by the one from Penlee, retired to Hugh Town with nine of the tanker's crew aboard, all Italians, having been on station for thirty and a half hours, possibly the longest continuous service performed by an Isles of Scilly lifeboat since its installation in 1837.

By Monday 20 March, the slick had increased until it measured thirty miles by eight, its stench quite plain at Truro, forty-eight miles away, and later as far afield as Newton Abbot, in Devon. Capt. Pastrengo Rugiati expressed an opinion that same day that his ship still had a 50/50 chance of survival, but fears had been expressed at government level that the *Torrey Canyon* might never be re-floated. Consequently, the Under Secretary for Defence (Navy), Mr Maurice Foley, flew to Plymouth and set up a co-ordinating headquarters at Mount Wise. It had been suggested that the ship and her remaining oil should be burnt, but even governments cannot legally set fire to private property without the owners' consent, and in this case the owners were still making strenuous efforts to save their ship.

On the Tuesday, the tugs *Utrecht, Titan, Stentur* and *Praia de Adrago* stood ready to pull their hearts out, and compressors poured high-pressure air into the damaged starboard tanks. There came a violent explosion in the engine-room, seven men were injured, another two blown off the ship into the sea, and a hole 18 ft square was blasted clean up through three decks just forward of the funnel. It was a terrifying experience for those on board and in nearby ships, for the wreck still contained at least 95,000 tons of oil and could remotely have exploded, destroying everything within a large radius. The tanker was immediately abandoned, the injured being transferred to the West Cornwall Hospital at Penzance, where Capt. Hans Stahl, the chief salvage officer, one of the two men blown overboard, was found to be dead. At least 30,000 tons of oil was promptly added to that already floating on the surface, covering an area thirty-five miles by twenty-two, and worse was to follow. At sea, nineteen ships sprayed continuously, the oil being now less than twelve miles from the Cornish beaches.

That Easter holiday was ruined for thousands of families. Meetings between salvage officials and the government went on throughout the night, troops were sent to the West Country, factories turned out detergent in quantities never seen before, and in a plastics

Opposite: Her hull broken in three places by the action of the sea, the bombed hull and burnt out hulk of the tanker *Torrey Canyon* on 30 March 1967, when she was abandoned as a total constructive loss, the largest and most damaging shipwreck in British waters.

factory near Liverpool men worked on the construction of 130 blocks of plastic foam, each measuring 30 ft long by 3 ft square, designed to support a boom to encircle the wreck and contain the oil. Meanwhile, in Devonport dockyard riggers worked on a special canvas skirt to hang beneath the boom, whilst on the cliffs at Lands End, look-out posts were established, reminiscent of the days when the country awaited the arrival of a different sort of seaborne enemy. On Good Friday the first of the oil came ashore at Sennen Cove, and every available boat that could hold a 45-gallon drum of detergent converged on the area. Easter Saturday and Sunday offered the salvage men two days in which to prepare for an all-out effort on Monday, the highest tide of the season. A second attempt to pull the *Torrey Canyon* clear of the rocks on Saturday succeeded in moving the vessel slightly, but nothing more, whilst Sunday's efforts ended in complete disaster.

At 7.45 pm on that Easter Sunday, half supported on compressed air, half on rock, battered by two severe gales during the previous week, weakened by the internal explosion and four tugs almost pulling her stern clean off, the *Torrey Canyon* broke in half abaft the bridge and oil simply gushed out. Twenty-four hours later the wreck lay in three pieces, with her bridge section awash. At least 80,000 tons of oil had by now been released, threatening hundreds of miles of the loveliest coastline and beaches in the country, immediately prior to its holiday season. It was a situation no country in the world had ever had to face, there was no experience and very few answers, and people found out as they went along how best to treat the 'black tide'. At sea, fifty-three major vessels were spraying night and day, whilst on land thousands of troops, sailors, airmen, firemen, cadet forces and volunteers used anything that would hold detergent, even down to watering cans! Well over half a million gallons of detergent were poured over the oil, but even this was insufficient.

Meanwhile, on the Seven Stones Reef, the three broken sections of the wreck still held nearly a third of the original cargo, and the decision was taken to set it alight. The Trinity House tender *Stella* moved the lightship off station, and an area within a 20-mile radius of the wreck was declared closed to all shipping. At 4 pm on Tuesday 28 March, 'Buccaneer' strike aircraft of the Royal Navy delivered the first thirty 1,000-1b bombs, followed by 'Hunter' aircraft of the Royal Air Force, which dumped 5,400 gallons of kerosene from wing drop-tanks, and flames were soon reaching a height of 500 ft, and smoke 8,000 ft. The following day more high explosive bombs were dropped, then napalm, and by Thursday morning it was all over. What had once been a ship was now only a burnt-out tangle of steel, the sea finally demolishing the wreck so that no part now shows above water. It had taken 200,000 lb of explosive, 11,000 gallons of kerosene and 3,000 gallons of napalm to destroy her — the most dramatic, spectacular and publicised wreck in the long history of Cornwall. Built by the Newport News Shipbuilding & Dry Dock Company in 1959, the *Torrey Canyon* had a gross tonnage of 38,562, 65,920 tons deadweight. During 1965 she had been 'jumboised' by the Sasebo Heavy Industries Co of Japan, who had cut her in half and added an extra 164 ft to her length, almost doubling her carrying capacity and increasing her deadweight tonnage to 118,285. With a draught of 51 ft, she was only a matter of 50 ft shorter than the old liner *Queen Elizabeth*. The Torrey Canyon has been in the news three times since the last visible part of her superstructure disappeared underwater. In 1982 her entire forepart, still intact, was refloated and converted into an oil storage barge, and shortly after two of the four blades of her huge phosphor-bronze propeller were removed by divers. One was lost overboard accidentally in 120m depth whilst being carried to Padstow, the other was landed at Hayle, the salvor subsequently being prosecuted.

Exactly how many ships have been lost on the Seven Stones Reef over the centuries will never be known. One author suggests 'only fourteen wrecks have been recorded on the reef'[1], another '257 for Scilly and the Seven Stones together between 1679 and 1923'[2] but this chapter alone, will mention the details of at least fifty and there have been many more. The earliest recorded wreck is that of the sixth rate, 22 gun English man o'war *Primrose*, which put to sea with the *Mayflower* in search of two Spanish frigates which were cruising in the area. In early March 1656 the *Mayflower* lost her main topmast in heavy weather off the Longships, and whilst Captain Sherwin of the *Primrose* was away from his ship arranging with Captain Bown to supply him with a spare, the *Primrose* drifted on to the Seven Stones. Although they managed to get her off, badly damaged she sank in 60 fathoms, sixteen men, two women and a child going down with the ship. When Trinity House were requested by the Admiralty to investigate the obstruction, they pronounced there had been no neglect either in the officers or company, the place where the *Primrose* miscarried being a rock not visible nor described in any part (chart) they could find. Another early wreck was the *Revenge* on 30 November 1674, from which only two of her seventeen crew were saved, followed by the 14-gun sloop HMS *Lizard*, Captain Siffon, wrecked with the loss of over one hundred men on 27 February 1748. The *Lizard* was a small vessel of 272 tons (bm), 92 ft long and 26 ft in the beam, and had been launched by Ewer at Bursledon on the River Hamble on 22 December 1744.

During the next one hundred years there must have been innumerable other wrecks here and as early at 1826 the government was being petitioned to place a light on the reef. Unfortunately, history has not recorded many of the names of ships lost here in the early

Belfast to Plymouth with a general cargo, the SS. *Longships* stuck the Seven Stones Reef and broke her back on 22 December 1939. Her crew of 27 were saved by the St. Mary's lifeboat RNLI *Cunard*

1800s, but we do know about the *Fortune*, lost while carrying a general cargo from London to Dublin. She struck the reef on 12 February 1802, her crew being picked up by a Yarmouth brig. Four pilots from Scilly attempted to save the derelict, but it sank beneath them, drowning two of the men. The British brig *Perseverence* was another of the early wrecks. Bound from Dublin to London, she struck during fog at 7 am on 14 November 1805, her crew rowing themselves to St Mary's. She was followed by an Exeter brig, *Reward*, on 6 November 1810, laden with oats and butter from Limerick, and by the *Hope* of Fowey on 5 May 1814. An unidentified schooner was seen to hit the 'Stones' on 16 January 1826, and on 29 October of the following year, the American ship *Susan* of Boston, Matanzas to Hamburg with logwood and cotton, struck in rough seas. Her crew were rescued by the Tresco pilot cutter *Hope*, except for one, a Negro who was drowned. The Dutch galliot *Twende Sodskende*, Bilbao to Copenhagen, also hit the reef late in 1827, sinking two miles off Bryher on 9 September. A brig, the *Joseph* of Sunderland, carrying pig-iron from Cardiff to London, was wrecked here on 18 November 1833, and in 1837 the barque *Golden Spring*, of and from London for Liverpool with general cargo, found the reef in fog on 16 May but was refloated at high water, a similar but less dramatic experience to that which befell the East Indiaman *Larkins* the following year.

It was 8 am on Sunday, 18 November 1838, when the *Larkins* hove-to between Scilly and Lands End to take on a pilot named Hicks. The pilot had no sooner gained the main deck than the vessel struck heavily three times, then floated clear, leaking badly. With the pumps unable to hold their own, Capt. Ingram, the passengers, and mail, were transferred to the pilot-cutter, the crew remaining aboard. Upon arrival at Penzance, Capt. Ingram hired fifty men, and they set off in boats to find the

The Panamanian Liberty ship *Mando* of 7,176 gross tons, which drove ashore on Golden Ball Bar, 21 January 1955, between Tresco & St. Martin's.

Indiaman. After a fruitless search lasting all one day and night, the men returned, and Capt. Ingram departed for Falmouth to consult Capt. Plumridge, who ordered HMS *Meteor*, a wooden paddle vessel, to find the *Larkins*. She was located between Falmouth and the Lizard, having already been taken in hand by a pilot, James of Coverack, who had recruited twenty-six local men to work the pumps. The *Larkins* reached Falmouth with 8 ft of water in her hold, and after going alongside Boyes cellars, discharged cases of indigo, silk and saltpetre from the lower hold.

The first petition for a light on the Seven Stones met with no success, but a second, supported by the Chamber of Commerce of Waterford, merchants from Liverpool and the British Channel ports in 1839, carried more weight. At a meeting held in Falmouth on 21 February 1840, it was declared that a light positioned on or near the reef would shorten the passage around Scilly by as much as thirty-six hours. As a result, a lightship appeared at St Mary's on 31 July 1841, was moored in position after considerable difficulties by the 20th and exhibited its first light on 1 September 1841, too late by nearly a year to have prevented the wreck, on 4 October 1840, of a Scilly-registered schooner, *Flying Fish*. Bound from Liverpool to Constantinople with general cargo, the schooner struck the rocks and nearly became a total loss, her crew being picked up by St Martins fishermen.

At first, the new lightship was in constant trouble, breaking her moorings and dragging out of position. On 25 November 1842 she was almost wrecked when the cable again parted and she drove over the reef, fortunately at high water. Her crew had evidently had enough, for they slipped the broken cable and set sail for New Grimsby, remaining there until 6 January the following year. In position again, she broke adrift within a matter of days, and in the March went clean over the reef for the second time.

In 1848, on 29 September, one of the lightship's two longboats was used to rescue the mate of the Barnstaple schooner *Caroline*; the sole survivor after his ship, carrying a coal cargo from Newport to Tarragona, had struck the reef in fog and foundered. The same longboat capsized in a squall and drowned two of the lightship's crew on 15 October 1851, whilst returning from Scilly with stores. Earlier that same year, on 23 April, the timely appearance of the barque *Mary Laing* had saved the crew of the Exeter brig *Amethyst*, carrying china clay from Teignmouth to Quebec, when she slipped off the rocks and sank six hours after striking in bad visibility.

As well as displaying a warning light, the Seven Stones Reef lightship also offered sanctuary to the crews of shipwrecked vessels, and the first arrival of these 'temporary guests' was in 1853, following the loss of the Maltese brig *Ambassador* on 12 June. Deep loaded with Cardiff coal, and bound for her Mediterranean home port, she struck and sank within half an hour. Thick fog also put the full-rigged Cape Horner *America* on the reef on 2 February 1854. Registered at St Johns, New Brunswick, this sixteen-month-old ship was carrying guano from Callao to Queenstown and London when she struck. Within the hour she had sunk, her crew being rescued by the Scilly boat *New Prosperous* and landed at St Ives. One of the many fishing-boat incidents on the reef occurred on 27 April 1859, when the Newlyn-owned *Fame* was caught in a severe ESE gale whilst attempting to reach Scilly for shelter. She capsized and sank in heavy seas just off the lightship and there were no survivors.

In 1860, the Seven Stones claimed the Sunderland barque *Punjab*. Commanded by Capt. Dale, the *Punjab* was carrying 300 tons of wool and hides from Algoa Bay to Amsterdam, when she hit the reef at 3.15 am on 14 September. With shattered bows and filling fast, she drifted clear to leeward, and it was whilst the vessel was being abandoned that the wife of one of the passengers, the Rev. Arbouset, was drowned as she clung to the rigging, too terrified to let go. Although a schooner passed close by the waterlogged longboat containing the rest of the passengers and crew, the lookout failed to see them and it was not until dawn that they were sighted and

rescued by the *Joshua and Mary* and landed at Falmouth. More 'temporary guests' appeared alongside the lightship in a boat on 18 September 1866, when the crew of five from the Glasgow schooner *Emilie* escaped after she was wrecked in fog. Bound from Poole to Runcorn, the vessel had heeled over and sunk within five minutes of striking the reef.

When another Sunderland barque, the *Cubana*, struck bows-on to the rocks on 25 April 1866, both her master, who should have been on watch at the time, and the mate, were below asleep in their bunks. Under the influence of a strong SE wind, the barque had been beating down Channel, having recently left Swansea for St Jago, Cuba, with sixteen crew, one passenger and a cargo of coal, iron, and mining gear. Her master rushed on deck after the impact but, apparently paralysed by fright, was quite unable to take command of the situation or himself. Taking matters into their own hands, the mate, nine of the crew and the passenger took to one of the boats and left the captain and six shipmates to perish. After a hard row, the lightship loomed up out of the haze and they were taken aboard. Next morning, when they were transferred to St Mary's by pilot cutter, they found they were not the only survivors to reach Scilly that day, the pilot cutter *Agnes* having previously landed Capt. McKeller and his crew from the *Ebgante* of Quebec. Bound from New York to Liverpool with oak, the *Ebgante* had been abandoned in a sinking condition on the 4th, when some 100 miles west of Scilly, and her crew had been taken off by the ship *Ferdinand* of Bremen before meeting up with the pilot cutter.

Following 1867, there was at least one wreck a year on the 'Stones', often more, right through until 1890. On 8 May 1868, the 135-ton brig *Gleaner* of Newport, William Prance master, on passage from Bilbao with iron ore, went missing off Land's End and was later known to have sunk some 30 miles NW by w of Land's End, presumably having hit the reef. An East Coast fishing lugger found her captain's writing desk, a meat safe, and other identifiable wreckage in the vicinity.

More visitors to the lightship, fourteen in all — which must have strained the resources of the vessel to its limits — appeared on 1 September 1869 after the master of the *Oxus*, John Dixon Wilson, mistook the 'Stones' light for the Longships and passed too close, a not uncommon occurrence. Loaded with 720 tons of rice from Akyab, Burma, this Dundee-registered ship of 536 tons register had left Queenstown with orders for London on 29 August. Between 8 and 10.30 pm on 31 August, following some confusion over identification of the three lights in sight, she struck the reef, then floundered on for a short distance before going down. By morning, only her main royal and sky-sail could be seen above the surface. Her crew had something of a struggle to reach the lightship, taking from 10.30 pm until 3.30 am to row the short distance between it and the wreck. Launched at Dundee in 1857, the *Oxus* was valued at £6,000.

In 1870, on 4 April, the *St Peterborg*, Glasgow to Rotterdam, struck part of a submerged wreck on the edge of the Seven Stones and immediately foundered, to be joined on 7 October by the timbers of the barque *Nelson* of Shields. After discharging coal and coke at Catagena, the 549-ton *Nelson*, registered at Fleetwood but technically owned in Shields, sailed from Aquias for the Tyne on 16 August with a cargo of pig-iron and esparto grass. All went well until 6 October, when she was running under foresail and reefed topsails before a strong SSW gale, accompanied by thick drizzling rain. At 3 o'clock in the afternoon, just as Capt. Henderson took over the deck watch, the barque hit either the South Stone or Flemish Ledge and lurched heavily, throwing everyone to the deck. Her gig was lowered but was caught by a breaking sea and drifted away with five men aboard but without either oars or tholepins. Both lifeboat and jolly-boat were jammed solid in their chocks, and with the sea lapping over the main deck, the remaining crew grasped what they could in the way of oars, casks and ladders and jumped overboard. Two minutes later, the ten-year-old *Nelson* went down by the bows, drowning her 50-year-old captain, his nephew and able seaman Moon. The occupants of the gig and five other survivors managed to reach the lightship.

In 1871, a seaman named Vincenzo Defelice was landed at St Martins by a pilot-gig after a remarkable escape from the wreck of the Spanish barque *Primos* on 24 June. This 600-ton vessel from Bilbao was carrying sugar from Havana to Falmouth for orders when she hit the rocks at 5 am. The first boat to be launched drifted away, a second manned by her captain and four crew capsized, after which the barque foundered, drowning all eleven crew except for Defelice who found himself alone in a stormy sea. He swam about for two hours, then found a floating hen-coop onto which he scrambled, remaining there for about an hour until he spotted the ship's figurehead. This life-sized female figure, now in the Valhalla collection at Tresco, kept him afloat for several more hours and when one of the ship's boats drifted close to him, he managed to get aboard and row to English Island Neck, from where he was rescued by pilots.

Although not a wreck incident, the barque *Athole* of London, Swansea to Cape Verde Islands with coal, has the doubtful honour of being the one and only ship to hit the Seven Stones lightship. This occurred on 30 January 1873, during a fine, clear afternoon, when the *Athole* ran alongside and caught her rigging on the lightship's bumpkin, carrying away her main and mizzen halyards and starboard light. On 3 February of the same year an unidentified brigantine foundered nearby in heavy seas. A French schooner was near enough to have rescued her crew but the master decided it was too dangerous to go close in, and all were left to drown. Another unidentified wreck, that of a full-rigged ship, occurred in December 1873, and during the following year, the 1,780 tons register *Rydall Hall* was fortunate in being taken in tow by the *Queen of the Bay* when dangerously close to the reef on 20 April, for which service the packet received £150 despite their tow sinking. Registered at Liverpool and outward bound on her maiden voyage for San Francisco with a general cargo, the *Rydall Hall* had lost almost all her head gear in a gale.

During 1875, two barques went on the rocks, the *Floresta* of Sunderland and the *Foscolo* of Naples. The 299-ton *Floresta* went ashore in fog at 4 am on 14 February and sank very quickly, her crew of ten being rescued by a St Malo lugger named *Josephine*, and landed at Falmouth. The 452-ton Italian vessel was more fortunate. After striking the rocks at 2 pm on 23 November, she managed to reach Crow Bar at Scilly, only to sink in the shallows from which she was later salvaged and raised. The *Floresta*, inward bound from Taganrog to Falmouth for orders, was loaded with wheat, while the *Foscolo* was carrying the odd mixture of bones and scrap iron from Montevideo to Dundee. A year later, on 13 November, the French schooner *Paul et Marie*, carrying a cargo of wheat, was dismasted after going ashore, and was eventually brought into Scilly as a derelict. The victim for 1877 was the *William Van Name*, an American barque of 700 tons net, which had left New York with a choice of calling at either Queenstown or Falmouth for orders. Capt. Cogniss chose the former and struck the reef at 3.45 am on 16 October. He and his crew of eleven were picked up and landed at Penzance by the schooner *Caroline* of Looe. Then there was the brig *Rosaire* of Nantes in 1879, with coal from Newport for Brest, which struck and went down on 26 February, four of her crew being picked up by the famous pilot-cutter *Queen*.

In relatively quick succession there followed an unidentified brig on 13 September 1884, the barque *Elizabeth Graham* of London, ashore but refloated and saved, 29 September 1885; and the 89-ton Plymouth schooner *Jane Sophia*, which was lost on 20 August 1887 after colliding with the steamer *Zenobia*, although her crew of five were saved.

Next to fall victim to the reef was the iron full-rigged ship *Barremman* of Glasgow, which hit on 9 July 1887 in rough foggy weather and sank without a single survivor from her crew of twenty-seven. She quickly went to pieces and next day hatch covers, a deckhouse and some loose wreckage ashore on St Martins were all

that remained of her. Owned by Robert Thomas of Glasgow, the *Barremman*, 1,399 tons net, had left South Shields for San Francisco loaded with coke, bricks, cement and pig-iron, under the command of Capt. Law. At the subsequent enquiry held at Glasgow in September, a charge of culpable negligence was made against mate Hayhar of the Seven Stones lightship for not going to their rescue.

The following decade saw a prodigious number of ships lost on the 'Stones', including three steamers. The first of these was the *Brighouse*, which had been launched by Palmer & Co at Newcastle in 1864. A three-masted iron steamer of 604 tons net, her dimensions were an overall length of 236 ft, beam 28.1 ft and depth 17.4 ft, and she was fitted with a 99 nhp engine. On passage from Bordeaux to Cardiff with pitwood, the *Brighouse* loomed out of the fog near the lightship on 12 December 1887, only to vanish again. An hour later, two lifeboats pulled alongside the lightship, and her crew identified themselves as having come from the Cardiff steamer. They were obliged to remain on the lightship for two weeks before being taken off, by which time the authorities had presumed the *Brighouse* lost with all hands, since one of her lifeboats and other wreckage had been washed ashore at Porthmeor, St Ives, three days after the wreck had occurred. At the enquiry which followed, the certificate of her master, Capt. Tregurtha of St Ives, was suspended for three months for his failure to observe proper precautions in fog.

Two more steamers went on the rocks in 1891, and the 77-ton schooner *Brenton* in the intervening years. The latter, carrying china clay, washed clear after hitting the Pollard Rock on 28 October 1890, and reached Falmouth full of water. Of the two steamers, the first was the 1,261-tons gross *Chiswick* of London, Cardiff to St Nazaire with coal, which went ashore in perfectly calm weather at 4.45 am on 5 February. When her engines were put full-astern, she lunged off into deep water and began to fill by the head, going down so quickly that only her port lifeboat floated clear. Her captain, the mate and nine men were drowned, but eight survivors were able to clamber onto the upturned boat and remained there for ten hours before being rescued by the lightship's longboat. Later that year, on 5 December, the *Merannio* of Leith, with 1,300 tons of iron ore on board and bound from Bilbao to Newport, also hit the Seven Stones but managed to reach St Ives, where she was beached in the harbour with a 10-ft hole in her bow. Although not directly attributable to the Seven Stones, a French steamer was lost on 19 February 1891 midway between Scilly and the reef. This was the *Trignac*, Newport to St Nazaire with coals, whose hull was so badly strained in rough seas that she sprang a leak and sank within five minutes after blowing up.

Despite warning rockets fired from the lightship on 1 October 1892, the 2,226 tons gross steamer *Camiola* of Newcastle continued on her course and went ashore at full speed, shaking violently from stem to stern with the impact. In the ensuing confusion, the engineer on watch drove her even further on the rocks when he put the engines to emergency 'full-ahead' instead of 'full-astern' and she commenced to fill. Her lifeboat lowering gear was in such a deplorable state, with fastenings and pins rusted and blocks seized, that it was impossible to get them clear at first. Eventually, using hammers and chisels, they were freed and pushed over the side. Owned by Chapman & Mills, the *Camiola* had sailed from Barry Docks and was bound for Malta with 3,400 tons of coal. A further sidelight on the character of her master was that, after reaching Penzance in the Trinity House tender *Alert*, Capt. Story and his officers made for the Union Hotel, leaving the crew to fend for themselves. At midnight, the disgruntled crew demanded to see the captain, who reluctantly advanced them two shillings each out of his own pocket. It was the second ship that Capt. Story had lost, the other one being off Nova Scotia two years earlier.

During the early hours of 5 July 1897, the steamer *Heathmore* of Liverpool ran full tilt into the Seven Stones, and at first there was every hope that she could be saved. Laden with 2,400 tons of iron-ore from Santander for Glasgow,

she floated clear at 8 am and was brought to anchor two miles clear of the reef with her crew pumping furiously. An offer of assistance from a passing steamer was declined, and only after the *Alert* arrived did Capt. A.F. Hird decide to go to St Mary's and telegraph Penzance for tugs. The steamer's crew pumped all that day but by evening, when it was obvious that they were fighting a losing battle, they took to their boats. Ten minutes later, the *Lady of the Isles* arrived, just in time to see the waterlogged steamer sink bows first into forty fathoms. Launched in 1883 by J. Key & Sons of Kinghorn, the *Heathmore* had only recently been sold to W. Johnston & Co of Liverpool by her former owners, the Heathmore Steamship Co.

Following the turn of the century, the Milford Haven steam trawler *Hydrangea* set out from her home port for fishing grounds off Scilly, but got off course and hit the reef at 10.30 pm on 15 June 1905. Filling fast, she was abandoned, and her crew were able to reach the lightship in their own punt. In 1908, the French crabber *St Louis* of Douarnenez struck and foundered on 20 June; a 180-ton Norwegian schooner, *Frau Mini Peterson*, was lost some distance off after collision on 3 August 1911, and later that year there was a tragic loss of life in the wreck of the steamer *Van Dyck*.

It was pitch dark and mountainous seas were running when the 1,132 tons gross *Van Dyck* of Antwerp, Valencia to Liverpool with oranges, onions and nuts, smashed into the Seven Stones at midnight on 6 December. Within minutes her engine-room was flooded to a depth of several feet and her fires swamped. The port boat was got away with eighteen men aboard but capsized, drowning the captain and thirteen of the crew, leaving only four men alive who scrambled back aboard. During the night the steamer floated off the rocks and had

Overleaf: The last victim of the Seven Stones to date, the Rumanian trawler and fish factory-ship *Rarau* stranded and became a total wreck on 29 September 1976. All 87 of her crew were taken off and saved when she broke in two.

drifted for some miles up-Channel when the four men still aboard were able to attract the attention of the steam collier *Ashtree*, which attempted a tow but found conditions too rough. The *Van Dyck* survivors then hastily assembled and launched a raft, reaching the *Ashtree* not long before the *Lyonesse* and *Greencastle* arrived and towed the derelict to Penzance, where she was beached.

When the reef claimed the Glasgow ship *Wendur* on 12 March 1912, the world lost one of its fastest sailing vessels. She held the record for the fastest passage between Newcastle and Valparaiso, and had been a regular visitor to

A Morlaix registered fishing vessel,the *Marie des Isles* went ashore on the island of Innisidgen, between Bar Point and Pelistry, filled and sank. She was later refloated and taken into Hugh Town harbour.

West Country ports, sailing from Plymouth with 2,900 tons of grain on her last voyage. She struck the Seven Stones twenty-three minutes after midnight, throwing the deck watch off their feet, and the apprentice at the helm clean over the top of the wheel. Five minutes later her main and mizzen masts broke off and collapsed, followed by the fore topmast, leaving the *Wendur* a crippled hulk. In the process of launching her two boats, the starboard one with ten men aboard was smashed, but its occupants were picked up by those in the port boat. Of the *Wendur's* total crew of twenty-one, three men were lost in the wreck. Built in 1884 by Connell & Co of Glasgow, the *Wendur*, of 2,046 tons gross, foundered on the southernmost rock of the group.

An 8,825 tons gross liner had a lucky escape on 26 May 1913. This was the Leyland Line's steamer *Armenian*, on passage from Rotterdam

to Cardiff in ballast, which struck the reef, got off in about five minutes and returned to Falmouth only slightly damaged. Another steamer, the *Toanui* of Glasgow, was lost on the reef without trace of survivors between 6-14 June 1913. A Penberth fisherman found a wooden box drifting off Tolpedn containing female clothing and jewellery, and next day a lifebelt marked 'Toanui—Glasgow' was found below Land's End, together with broken boats and wreckage.

A destroyer of 975 tons, HMS *Pincher,* was totally wrecked on the Seven Stones on 24 July 1918; the steamer *Cornish Coast* stranded there on 28 November 1924 but survived to run down and sink the steamer *Fagerness* off Trevose Head on 17 March 1926; and a Clyde Shipping Co steamer, the *Longships*, Belfast to Plymouth with general cargo, stranded and broke her back on the rocks on 22 December 1939.Nine years later the steamer *Duke of Sparta* became one of the few modern steamers to have escaped after stranding on the reef, when she was successfully refloated on 19 April 1948. Dense fog on 6 October 1949 put the motor-vessel *Fantee* of Liverpool, belonging to the Elder Dempster Line, on the rocks, her crew of fifty-eight officers and men all being rescued by the Scilly launches *Kittern* and *Golden Spray*. She, too, broke her back and settled down with her cargo floating out, covering the surface with palm kernels, palm oil, cocoa, rubber, hardwoods, cotton, coffee beans and copra. Forty three years after the loss of the *Fantee*, whole trunks of hardwood trees are still being salvaged from the wreck, and utilised for house decoration and furniture.

Prior to the *Torrey Canyon*, the last wreck on the Seven Stones Reef had been that of the Panamanian steamer *Punta*, Capt. Mathiasso. Carrying phosphate rock from Spain to Portishead and Bristol, she struck over two miles from the lightship on 22 July 1955 and was abandoned by her crew of twenty-four. The St Mary's lifeboat was again in constant attention, returning only after completing a fourteen-hour vigil. Before tugs could begin to pull the *Punta* clear, she had filled and sunk in fifteen fathoms, damaged beyond all hopes of salvage. A newspaper report at the time stated that tugs pulled her off but, in fact, she came off the reef and sank of her own accord.

Since the *Torrey Canyon* the Seven Stones have claimed two more victims, the Constanza registered Rumanian fish-factory trawler *Rarau*, wrecked on 29 September 1976, and the French trawler *Le Resolu*, lost on 17 March 1980. All 84 of the Rumanian crew on board the *Rarau* were saved before she broke in two. When boats from Scilly arrived alongside, and their occupants commenced to 'rescue' items of value from the bridge, the captain ordered them to leave immediately. Knowing that the ship would never be saved, and at high water would be partly submerged, the Scillonians produced copies of 'Playboy' magazine and gave them to the captain, who promptly lost all interest in anything else, and with a wave of his hand agreed they could help themselves – a very good bargain indeed!

DERELICTS & DEEP-WATER WRECKS
CHAPTER ⑧

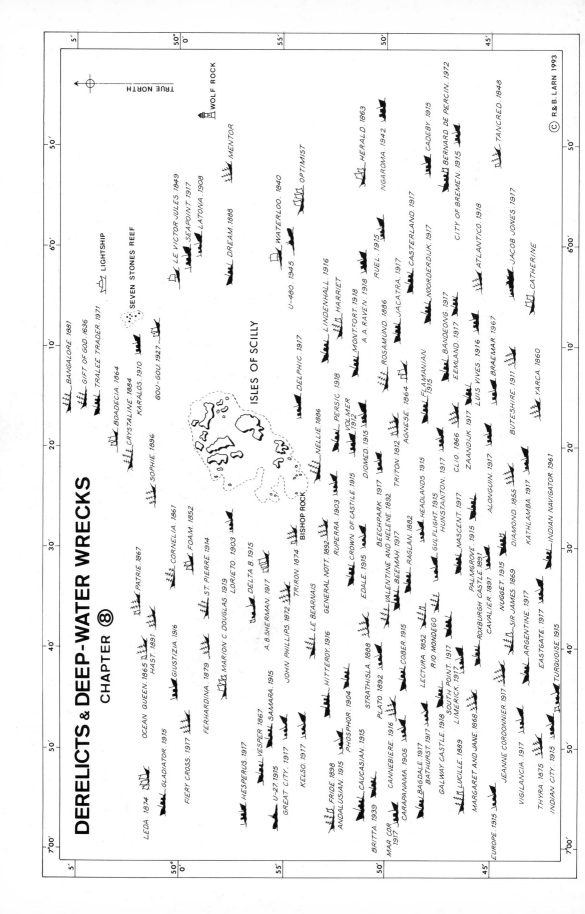

© R&B. LARN 1993

TRUE NORTH

WOLF ROCK

LIGHTSHIP

SEVEN STONES REEF

ISLES OF SCILLY

BISHOP ROCK

LEDA. 1874
GLADIATOR. 1915
OCEAN QUEEN. 1865
HAST. 1891
PATRIE. 1867
BANGALORE. 1881
GIFT OF GOD. 1636
TRALEE TRADER. 1971
GIUSTIZIA. 1916
FIERY CROSS. 1917
CORNELIA. 1861
BOADECIA. 1864
CRYSTALINE. 1884
KARALOS. 1910
GOU-GOU. 1927
LE VICTOR-JULES. 1849
SEAPOINT. 1917
FERHARDINA. 1879
FOAM. 1852
SOPHIE. 1896
LATONA. 1908
ST. PIERRE. 1914
MENTOR
MARION C. DOUGLAS. 1919
LORIETO. 1903
DREAM. 1888
HESPERUS. 1917
DELTA B. 1915
A.B.SHERMAN. 1917
WATERLOO. 1840
VESPER. 1867
SAMARA. 1915
JOHN PHILLIPS. 1872
TRI-IRON. 1874
U-480. 1945
OPTIMIST
U-27. 1915
GREAT CITY. 1917
LE BEARNAIS
DELPHIC. 1917
KELSO. 1917
GENERAL NOTT. 1892
NELLIE. 1886
PERSIC. 1918
LINDENHALL. 1916
HARRIET
FRIDE. 1898
ANDALUSIAN. 1915
PHOSPHOR. 1904
HITTEROY. 1916
RUPERRA. 1903
CROWN OF CASTLE. 1915
VOLMER. 1912
MONTFORT. 1918
A. A. RAVEN. 1918
RUEL. 1915
CAUCASIAN. 1915
EDALE. 1915
DIOMED. 1915
ROSAMUND. 1886
NGAROMA. 1942
BRITTA. 1939
STRATHISLA. 1888
BEECHPARK. 1917
VALENTINE AND HELENE. 1892
TRITON. 1812
JACATRA. 1917
CASTERLAND. 1917
MAR COR. 1917
PLATO. 1892
COBER. 1915
BEEMAH. 1917
RAGLAN. 1882
AGNESE. 1864
FLAMANIAN. 1915
NOORDERDIJK. 1917
CADEBY. 1915
CANNEBIERE. 1916
LECTURA. 1852
GULFLIGHT. 1915
HEADLANDS. 1915
BANDEONG. 1917
CARAPANAMA. 1905
RIO MONDEGO
HUNSTANTON. 1917
EEMLAND. 1917
BERNARD DE PERCIN. 1972
BAGDALE. 1917
BATHURST. 1917
SOUTH POINT. 1917
NASCENT. 1917
CLIO. 1866
ZAANDIJK. 1917
LUIS VIVES. 1916
CITY OF BREMEN. 1915
GALWAY CASTLE. 1918
LIMERICK. 1917
LUCILLE. 1889
PALMGROVE. 1915
ALONQUIN. 1917
ATLANTICO. 1918
MARGARET AND JANE. 1868
ROXBURGH CASTLE. 1893
BRAEMAR. 1967
CAVALIER. 1891
NUGGET. 1915
DIAMOND. 1855
BUTESHIRE. 1911
JACOB JONES. 1917
EUROPE. 1915
JEANNE CORDONNIER. 1917
SIR JAMES. 1869
KATHLAMBA. 1917
CATHERINE
VIGILANCIA. 1917
ARGENTINE. 1917
YARCA. 1860
TANCRED. 1848
THYRA. 1875
EASTGATE. 1917
INDIAN NAVIGATOR. 1961
INDIAN CITY. 1915
TURQUOISE. 1915
HERALD. 1863

Deep water wrecks and derelicts

There are many wreck incidents connected with the Isles of Scilly which have no place in the preceding chapters, simply because they occurred some distance from land. These distances vary considerably, and the vessels concerned may have been lost by fire or collision, foundered due to stress of weather, been torpedoed, scuttled, leaked, capsized or just fallen to pieces. All, however, had some connection with the islands, indirect though it may have been, usually because their crews landed there, wreckage was washed ashore, or ships were found derelict by the island's pilots or fishermen.

Many such derelicts have been found off the Isles of Scilly, some burnt to the waterline, others with several feet of water in their holds, some with only a few inches and virtually undamaged. Such vessels, successfully towed to safety in St Mary's Roads, represented considerable sums of money to the salvors, and local pilots would make almost superhuman efforts to save a derelict when others had failed. On 6 August 1849, *Victor Jules*, a Nantes lugger, Capt. Ridal, France to Mumbles for orders, was towed into the roads, waterlogged and derelict. She was thought to have struck the Runnelstone or Seven Stones Reef, and it was not until her crew had been landed at Gloucester that their story became known. Her cargo of flour was auctioned off locally on 13 August, and the vessel sold.

A similar incident concerned the Bridgwater schooner *Boadicea*, picked up on 27 November 1864 by a St Agnes pilot cutter.

With the pilot boat tied astern to assist in steering, the derelict having lost her rudder, she reached St Mary's safely. It was eventually established from her owners that she had sailed from Newfoundland, and the pilots involved received a total of £530 salvage money in return for saving a vessel and cargo worth £1,763.

Instances of a master being found guilty of needless abandonment must be rare, but such was the case with the *Margaret and Jane*, a 324-ton barque registered at Scilly. She sailed from Cardiff on 18 November 1868 with 520 tons of coal for Alicante, but although her papers showed John Stephens as master, it was in name only, the owner's son, David Hughes, actually being in charge. He had no certificate and was quite unqualified to act as master, having signed on as bo'sun and purser. Moreover, the barque put to sea inadequately caulked and leaked from the moment of sailing, carried an unseaworthy quarterboat and had no spare washers for the bilge pumps. When 120 miles from the Isles of Scilly, she met bad weather and turned back with one pump choked and out of commission. When the *Inez* of Sunderland hove in sight, the officers of the *Margaret and Jane* tried to lower the longboat but stove in some planks, whereupon the *Inez* sent over her own boat and took off the master, the owner's son and two other men. The rest of the crew, quite unaware that a distress signal had been flying from their own masthead, at first refused to leave their ship and were confident that, with only 27 in of water in the hold, there was every chance of saving her. Eventually, however, they obeyed the master's orders to abandon her, but assured him that she would probably be in Scilly before the *Inez* reached Swansea. That same day, the Scilly pilot-cutter *Ezra* found the derelict, took her in tow, and reached Crow Sound without even touching the pumps. At the enquiry held at Caernarvon, the master had his certificate suspended for twelve months, the court expressing their regret that they had no power to punish Hughes who had virtually dominated proceedings on board. Some months later, on 8 April 1869, the sailing-ship *Sir James* was abandoned to the south-west of the islands after a sudden squall had carried away her masts. She was then on her way to Madras from Hartlepool with cargo of iron and coal. Her distress signals were sighted simultaneously by a French schooner and the steamer *Atlantic*, the former taking off the crew and landing them at Scilly, while the latter took the derelict in tow and reached Falmouth.

A Danish ship, the *Thyra*, was found abandoned some distance west of Scilly by the Liverpool-owned *Hoang Ho* on 30 January 1875. On passage from Philadelphia to Copenhagen with petroleum, the *Thyra* had apparently encountered a severe gale since her main and foremasts, jib-boom and boats had all gone overboard. Four seamen and the chief mate of the *Hoang Ho* boarded her, rigged jury sail and made Falmouth seven days later. A year earlier, on 14 February 1874, a German brig had also sailed into Falmouth to land the crew of the abandoned 326-ton three-masted schooner *Leda* of Stettin. Five days later, the steamer *Flandre*, Troon to Bayonne, came into the harbour with storm damage and reported that she had at one time had the *Leda* in tow, but rough seas had parted the hawsers. The derelict was located again on 20 February by Falmouth pilots, but they were unable to do anything with her and it was not until three Scilly pilot cutters got lines aboard that she was worked into St Mary's and saved. It was not at all unusual for steamships to pick up derelicts whilst on passage; the *Gladiator*, for example, found the German brigantine *Gerhardina* in this condition with 5 ft of water in her hold on 13 January 1879. She eventually succeeded in getting the vessel to Scilly, but the fate of the missing crew was never determined. By an odd coincidence, a steamer named *Gladiator* was sent to the bottom by a German submarine on 19 August 1915 when fifty miles NW of the Bishop, but was not the same one that had saved the *Gerhardina*.

In 1884, it took the combined efforts of four pilot boats and the Governor's private yacht, *Surprise,* to get the barque *Crystaline* to New Grimsby harbour. She was first sighted apparently in distress three miles north of St Martins by Douglas Skinner, a Trinity pilot on 16

November. The *Crystaline* of Liverpool, an iron-hulled vessel, was found to have been abandoned, her forward compartments flooded and water still pouring in through holes in her bows, the obvious result of a collision. When close to Scilly under tow, her bows went under water and she would have foundered but for the timely assistance of local boats. Such derelicts adrift on the high seas were a serious navigational hazard, and when the 273-ton brig *Lucille*, carrying casks and tallow to Falmouth for orders, was in collision with a steamer on 27 November 1889 sixty miles SW of the Bishop, four tugs were sent out to locate her. For three days the Falmouth tugs, *Emperor, Eagle, Armine,* and *Triton* searched the area assisted by the gunboat *Pelican* and another warship, and it was only when wreckage which included casks and tallow was sighted that the *Lucille* was presumed to have sunk and the search was called off. Owned by W. Williams of Newport, the 117-ft long *Lucille* had been built and launched by Yeo of Prince Edward Island in 1874.

Although the steamer *Cavalier* of Newcastle was sighted and reported as derelict sixteen miles WSW of the Western Rocks in 1891, a long and tedious search proved fruitless, the vessel apparently having sunk in the meantime. The *Indian Prince* had reported sighting her, with a heavy list to starboard, on 20 December after arrival at Rotterdam, and her owners, Walter Scott & Co of Newcastle, confirmed that she was homeward bound from Odessa to Falmouth for orders. The same day that the *Indian Prince* reported the derelict, a bunk head-board was washed ashore at Scilly from the wreck, and a glass and decanter rack marked 'SS Cavalier' found near Land's End was identified as having come from the chief officer's cabin. Nothing more of ship or crew was ever found, and the 1,197 tons net vessel, launched in 1878 by Doxfords of Sunderland, was declared a total loss.

As the 1800s came to a close and steamers became predominant on the world's shipping routes, so the numbers of derelicts fell sharply, but they still occurred, and two such instances off the Scillies were the barque *Sophie* in 1896, and the *Marion C. Douglas* in 1919. At first, the case of the *Sophie* appeared to offer a mystery equal to that of the *Mary Celeste* of 1872, at least until her crew turned up at Gibraltar on 20 December aboard the British steamer *Glenmore*. A Norwegian barque, the *Sophie* of Frederikstad, carrying anthracite from Swansea, was sighted on 15 December wallowing dismasted in heavy seas, four miles north of Shipman Head. Ten local men put out in a gig and found her derelict apart from a well-fed dog. The cabin table was laid as for a meal, there was half-prepared food in the galley, still warm, and the ship's clock was wound up and ticking. Assisted by Tresco and St Martins gigs, the *Lady of the Isles* and the St Mary's lifeboat, *Henry Dundas*, the barque was towed the four and a half miles to New Grimsby and anchored. The *Marion G. Douglas*, a wooden, three-masted schooner from Fox River, Nova Scotia, was also found derelict in less dramatic circumstances in December 1919 and successfully towed to Scilly. This 491-ton schooner, which had been launched by Hatfield in 1917, was close to her destination, Le Havre, when she was abandoned.

Amongst the hundreds, if not thousands of vessels which come under the heading of 'deepwater wrecks' off the Isles of Scilly, it is possible to mention but a small percentage. The American brig *Triton*, Boston to Liverpool foundered a few miles offshore on 13 May 1802, when her master and four crew drowned; a new pilot cutter, the 25-ton *Waterloo* shipped a heavy sea whilst off the islands and sank on Christmas Day 1840; 4 April 1848 saw the sixteen-year-old Sunderland brig *Tancred* of 350 tons sink in deep water after developing a leak, Capt. Oliver, the sole survivor being rescued by the schooner *Merlin* and landed at St Mary's. In 1852, the schooner *Foam* went down on 16 April, and the 40-ton sloop-rigged *Lectura* of Salcombe on 10 January 1852, lost with her cargo of oranges after a collision in which one of her five crew was drowned. An Irish schooner, the *Catherine* of Cork, with oats from Kinsale for London, filled and sank when her pumps were unable to cope with a leak on

8 February 1854; the *Diamond* of Swansea was lost on 30 October 1855; a brigantine, the *Mentor*, laden with copper ore, sank after hitting the Wolf Rock during fog on 18 May 1856; and the Yankee cotton ship *Yarca* was destroyed by fire in 1869.

News of the loss of the *Yarca* reached Falmouth on 3 April via the Neopolitan brigantine *W. E. Routh*. Her master reported that, whilst off the Scillies the previous afternoon, they had met up with the *Yarca* ablaze from stem to stern, and had kept watch on her until 4 am when three masts collapsed and a schooner appeared on the scene. This was the *Express* of Shoreham, which already had the *Yarca's* thirty-six crew on board. A wooden ship of 1,262 tons, the *Yarca*, under the command of Capt. Taylor, had left Liverpool for Bombay with steam coal for the Indian Station bunkers, but leaked so badly in the Irish Sea that the crew asked to be allowed to take to the boats. The captain refused, saying he intended to investigate the leak first, also a peculiar sulphurous smell which had been apparent in the cabin for some time. No sooner had the tarpaulins been rolled back and the wooden hatch covers removed than flames shot skyward, setting fire to the sails and rigging. The *W. E. Routh* reported that shortly after she left, the *Yarca*, valued at £15,000, rapidly sank. Somewhere north of the islands, two railway locomotives lie on the seabed amongst the wreckage of the *Cornelia* of Portland USA, lost along with a part-cargo of railway sleepers and coal from Greenock to Santos. She was striving desperately to reach Scilly with a serious leak when she sank on 4 April 1861. In 1863, the British schooner *Herald*, dismasted and damaged by storm fifteen miles west of the Bishop, would almost certainly have foundered but for the intervention of the wooden screw frigate HMS *Highflyer*, which towed her to the safety of the roads.

As the years passed, ships continued to be lost in deep water in apparently ever increasing numbers, although a peak was reached during the late 1860s. In 1864, the French schooner *Agnese* was sent to the bottom after collision with the *Circassian* of London on 5 January. The master of the badly damaged *Circassian*, Capt. Smith, died two days after the incident. A British barque, the *Ocean Queen* of Bristol went down on 17 May 1965, fourteen miles NNW of Scilly; another brig on 23 March 1866, the *Harriet* of Ardrossan; *Clio*, a full-rigged ship, on 1 July 1866, and the paddle steamer *Vesper*, on 19 January 1867.

The latter has rather an unusual story, since she was on passage from the Clyde to Bahia, in Brazil, where the 80-ton vessel was to serve as a passenger river boat under the name *Leito Cunha*. Commanded by Capt. Samuel Lindsay, the *Vesper* left Glasgow on 3 January, but by 18 January had only five or six days bunkers left, having encountered severe gales most of the way. However, this was of no real consequence since it was the intention to steam down to warmer latitudes, then sail the rest of the way to South America. When off Scilly at noon on 19 January there was a sickening crash and, without warning, the vessel broke clean in two. The drifting sections were flung against each other time after time, but watertight bulkheads fortunately kept them afloat. Soon after the accident, the Danish steamer *Vigilant*, Dublin to Bayonne, hove in sight and rescued the crew, though three had already been drowned in the wreck.

A Norwegian brig, the *Patrie*, carrying linseed from Odessa to Falmouth, was running before the wind after her cargo had shifted when she collided with the Norwegian barque *Vulcan* of Riisder on 17 March 1867, the *Patrie* sinking only a few miles NW of the Bishop. The *John Philips*, a Glasgow full-rigger, sprang a leak and sank off-shore on 9 June 1872; and the coal-laden brig *Triron* of Cardigan foundered near the Western Rocks on 16 April 1874. And in 1882 a steamer, the *Raglan* of Cardiff, owned by J. Cory & Sons, sank in three minutes after a collision, her boilers exploding and tearing up half the deck as she went under. The vessel with which she collided was another steamship, the *P. A. Vagliano*, sister-ship to the *Spyridion Vagliano* lost on the Manacles reef off Falmouth on 8 February 1890.

Other losses in the area included the 40-year-old wooden barque *Bangalore*, which capsized and sank twenty-five miles north of Scilly on 4 March 1881; the Swansea brigantine *Rosamund*, carrying phosphate from Sombrero to Gloucester, on 7 January 1886; the *Nellie*, another brigantine, on 26 March 1886 after striking a rock near the Bishop and going to pieces in ten minutes; the Penzance steamer *Dream*, after springing a bad leak between the Wolf Rock and Scilly on 5 March 1888; and the *Roxburgh Castle*, a Newcastle-registered steamer, after colliding south-west of Scilly on 13 March 1891 with the *British Peer*. Another steamer lost the following year was the *Plato*, which suffered a broken propeller shaft on 29 February, water leaking back up the stern tube until she foundered, despite attempts by her company sister-ship, the *J. W. Taylor*, to take her in tow. Launched at Newcastle by A. Leslie in 1878, the *Plato* was owned by a subsidiary of the Lamport & Holt Line. The Norwegian brigantine *Hast* of Arendal, Cardiff to Newhaven with coal, sprang a leak and sank fifteen miles NW of the islands on 22 April 1891, her crew being rescued by the Porthleven lugger *Harbinger*, while *Le Bearnais*, a French barque in ballast, was run down and sunk six miles west of the Bishop by the steamer *Llanberis* on 10 March 1893.

Collision, which accounted for so many of these losses, also terminated the career of two barques on 2 March 1892, when the *General Nott*, bound from Chile with nitrates, almost cut the French barque *Valentine & Helene* clean in half twenty miles from land. The Frenchman sank so quickly that her master, Capt. Jonajean, leapt overboard wearing only his night-shirt. Her crew were picked up by the badly damaged *General Nott*, and for sixteen and a half hours the two crews managed to keep her afloat, pumping furiously until, when some 15 miles wsw of the Bishop, a steamer, the *Barden Tower* of Glasgow, came alongside and took them off. She then took the barque in tow but late that same evening she rolled over and sank.

So the long list of casualties continues, the brig *Fride* of Gottenburg foundered at sea in

August 1898; the new river gunboat *Loretio*, on delivery to the Peruvian government, sank on 25 May 1903 when close to Scilly; the *Ruperra* of Cardiff, Barry to Port Said with coal, was cut completely in half and sunk at midnight on 29 July 1903, after being run down by the 3,400-ton British cruiser HMS *Melampus*. Another British steamer, the *Phosphor*, was found capsized west of Scilly and taken in tow by the *Birkhall*, only to sink on 13 July 1904; the *Carapanama* was lost on New Years Day 1905; the transatlantic liner *Latona*, of Dundee, on 20 May 1908, and the *Buteshire* in 1911. The *Latona* sank near the Wolf Rock after being rammed by the Sunderland steamer *Japanic*. Carrying forty-five crew, four passengers, twelve cattlemen, steers and a general cargo, the *Latona* kept stopping due to fog, and was not under way when the *Japanic* loomed out of the murk and struck her amidships. When the crew and passengers were mustered after rescue, there were four more than could be accounted for, the additions being stowaways who appeared only as the ship was sinking. Although there was no loss of human life in this incident, all 310 steers were drowned, their carcasses coming ashore along the south coast of Cornwall and Scilly.

On 29 March 1911, the master of the steamer *Duva* wrote in his log, 'I saw the four-masted barque *Buteshire* of Glasgow take her departure from the list of ships this day, at about 3.0 am, abandoned, on fire and full of water. We stopped and boarded her but had to get off pretty quickly. About ten minutes later she foundered, but I took a snapshot of her before she left, position about 28 miles SW of the Longships'. So ended the career of the 1,910-ton *Buteshire*, which had begun in July 1888 when she was launched by Birrells for the Shire Line, the first of two four-masted barques commissioned by Law & Co. She had loaded coal at Newcastle for Valparaiso, arriving after a

The four-masted barque *Buteshire,* on fire, full of water sinking 28 miles SW of the Longships and off Scilly, 29 March 1911. She had been abandoned two days earlier, this photograph being taken by the master of the SS. *Duva*, who witnessed her go down.

passage of sixty-one days. From there she proceeded to Pisagua and loaded nitrates, leaving for home on 18 November. A serious leak developed on 19 March and for the next eight days the crew, including the captain's wife, toiled continuously at the pumps. On the morning of 27 March, they were some 100 miles west of Brest and, convinced that his ship would sink any minute, Capt. Purdie signalled the steamer *Ardeola*, the first ship they had sighted, and all hands were taken off the barque. But the *Buteshire* remained afloat, was reported by the steamer *Milton* in position 48°47'N, 07°19'W, waterlogged and abandoned, but with lights still burning in the cabin and galley. She had been a very fast sailer in her day, reaching Hamburg from Iquique in 110 days in 1897, and Sydney from Hamburg in ninety-six days during 1898.

Of the many wrecks lying in deep water around the islands, the majority occurred during World War I. Merchant ships sailed alone and unarmed for the early part, making the busy shipping lanes in the vicinity of Hartland Point on the north coast of Cornwall, and Bishop Rock, a submarine commander's paradise. Exactly how many were lost here due to enemy action will never be known, for even the official records are hopelessly incomplete. On the very first day of the war Scillonians had the excitement of seeing the British cruisers HMS *Doris* and *Isis* capture and bring in two prize ships, the three-masted schooner *Bolivar* carrying hides and tallow, and the *Roland*, of Bremen, laden with tobacco and coffee from New Orleans. Both ships were deprived of their sails to prevent escape, but four of the *Bolivar's* crew commandeered a small open boat and put to sea. Some weeks later it was learnt that the steamer *New Pioneer*, owned by the Co-operative Wholesale Society, had arrived in the Mersey with the four men aboard, having picked them up in St Georges Channel, exhausted and without either food or water.

As the war progressed, so the numbers of sinkings increased ten-fold. Between 27 January and 18 February 1915, nine vessels were torpedoed or sunk by scuttling charges, and in March

one submarine, the *U-29*, sank three steamers, the *Headlands* of Liverpool, 2,988 tons gross, the *Indian City* of Bideford, 4,645 tons gross, and the *Andalusian* of Liverpool, 2,349 tons gross. The submarine commander was Otto Weddigan who, in the *U-9*, had previously sunk the armoured cruisers HMS *Cressey*, *Aboukir* and *Hogue* on 22 September 1914. The *Headlands*, in ballast, was ordered to stop and her crew to take to their boats, and she was so close inshore when the submarine torpedoed her that school children, watching from the heights of St Mary's, cheered and clapped, thrilled by the explosion and smoke. She floated for some hours but sank less than a mile southeast of the Bishop after a drifter, a motor-boat and the packet *Lyonesse* had all attempted a tow. Less than two months old, the *Indian City* of Bideford, bound from Galveston to the UK with cotton and spelter, had a Chinese crew who tried the patience of the submarine commander, making him wait whilst they put on their best clothes and packed their bags before manning the boats! No sooner had they got clear than a single torpedo ripped open her engine-room, and she caught fire. The *Andalusian* was thirty-five miles from the Bishop when ordered to stop, but her captain headed for Scilly in an attempt to outrun the U-boat. However, she was soon overhauled and forced to be abandoned, the Germans boarding her and taking all instruments, cutlery, and charts before scuttling her. The *U-29* did not enjoy her victories for long, being depth-charged and lost with all hands on 26 March 1915 in the North Sea.

The 3,500-ton steamer *Flaminian* was sunk by gunfire on 29 March 1915, the 4,505-ton *Crown of Castile* the following day, and on 1 May a submarine attacked the steamers *Edale*, *Europe* and *Gulflight*. The *Edale*, of 3,110 tons, took two torpedoes and nine shells, proving difficult to sink, as did the *Europe*, a French vessel of 2,026 tons gross carrying a cargo of coal. She was stopped three miles NW of the Bishop and absorbed twenty high-explosive shells without showing any sign of sinking. In sheer desperation, having spent over an hour on the surface

dealing with one merchantman, the submarine's commander fired a precious torpedo at her, whereupon the *Europe* folded up and sank.

The torpedoing of the *Gulflight* proved to be a bad mistake on the part of the Germans and caused them considerable embarrassment as she was American owned, and the US at that time was neutral. Carrying naphtha from Port Arthur, Texas, her home port, for Rouen, the *Gulflight* was stopped west of the Bishop and hit by one torpedo, whereupon her crew abandoned ship by jumping overboard, and three of them were drowned. The captain, a naturalised German named Gunther, died of heart failure on the bridge of the naval patrol vessel *Iago*. Her survivors were picked up by naval patrol vessels, and she was still afloat next day, with her bows under water. The Lowestoft drifters, *Premier*, *Diadem*, *Primrose*, *Dusty Miller* and *All's Well* took her in tow and, taking two days to cover eight miles, eventually got her into St Mary's Roads. While she was at anchor in the shallows, barrels of naphtha drifted out of the huge hole in her bows, and the government offered a reward of ten shillings for every barrel recovered. Built at Camden, NJ, in 1914, this 5,189-tons gross ship, owned by the Gulf Refining Co, was eventually towed to Le Havre with a

Torpedoed off the Bishop Rock in May 1915, the American oil tanker *Gulflight* was towed into St Mary's Roads and saved. Her captain died of heart failure on the bridge, and three crew actually jumped overboard and drowned when she was hit.

'scratch crew' from amongst the islanders, each of whom received £25 for the trip.

Other war losses included the Belgian steam fishing-vessel *Delta B* of 220 tons, sunk on 2 June 1915; the steamer *Cober*, 3,060 tons, on 21 August 1915; the steamer *Ruel*, 4,029 tons and the *Palmgrove*, 3,100 tons on the same day, and the *Diomed*, 4,672 tons, the following day. The *Cober*, Capt. Peterfield, made a dash for it when ordered to heave-to, and successfully eluded the submarine's gunfire for an hour before several direct hits brought her to a standstill and forced her crew to abandon. One torpedo was fired into her port side, and she sank very quickly. A similar fate befell the *Ruel*, Capt. Henry Storey, which was chased for an hour before one shell hit her stern, passing clean through, and another exploded on the bridge. After the crew had taken to the boats, the submarine closed the range and when within 150 yd its crew opened fire on the survivors with small arms, wounding many of the defenceless men. As the submarine departed it was noticed she had *U-23* painted on one side of her conning tower, and *U-26* on the other, so that her true identity was never established.

The West Hartlepool Steam Navigation Co's *Lindenhall*, 4,003 tons, built by the Irving S.B. Co in 1900, was attacked seven miles offshore on 1 November 1916 but survived. On 22 February 1917 a convoy of eight Dutch steamers, which had left Falmouth in company only the previous day, were attacked by the *U-3*, which sent six of the eight to the bottom. It was a beautifully sunny day, with the sea like a millpond, when three of the ships were hit by torpedoes in a matter of minutes, the others being stopped and sunk by scuttling charges. Remarkably, not a single life was lost, and the combined crews in twenty-eight boats, accompanied by the St Agnes lifeboat, made quite a spectacle as they reached St Mary's. For this particular service, each member of the lifeboat crew was awarded a special medal, struck by the Netherland section of the League of Neutral Countries. The six vessels lost were the *Jacatra*, 5,373 tons; the *Gaasterland*, 3,917 tons; the *Noorderdijk*, 7,166 tons; the *Eemland*, 3,700 tons, and the *Zaandijk*, 4,189 tons. The *Medado*, 5,874 tons, reached Falmouth, and the *Ambon* of Amsterdam, 3,598 tons, put into Plymouth with only slight damage.

By 1917, the majority of merchantmen were armed with a 'stern-chaser' gun, and although these were often ineffectual due to their vintage or small calibre, they did at least give the crews something with which to hit back. At the same time, they brought to an end the merciful practice of submarines stopping vessels and allowing the crews to escape unharmed. Ships were now sent to the bottom without warning, and the monthly tonnage lost in the western approaches reached immense proportions. The entire crew from a Portuguese steamer landed on the islands on 12 March 1917, to be followed next day by two boatloads of men from the American steamer *Algonquin*. The crew of another American ship, the *Vigilancia* of Wilmington, 4,115 tons, came ashore on 1 April, and later a total of eighteen survivors from the steamers *Argentine* and *Hunstanton*. The latter, ex-*Werdenfels*, 4,505 tons, had been requisitioned by the Admiralty earlier in the war and re-registered at London. A Yarmouth fishing-boat's crew reached the Sound on 25 April 1917, an unidentified steamer's crew numbering forty on 27 April, another steamer's crew on 8 May, and men from the Australian steamer *Limerick,* ex-*Rippington Grange*, 6,827 tons, built by Workham Clark & Co of Belfast in 1898, soon afterwards.

On 2 June, crews from the torpedoed steamers *Bagdale* of Whitby, 3,045 tons, and *Bathurst* of Liverpool, 2,821 tons, reached the Isles of Scilly in their own lifeboats; as did Frenchmen from the *Jeanne Cordonnier,* sunk on 31 May, and an Italian crew on 3 June. Two ships were towed into the roads on 18 June with gaping holes made by torpedoes in their sides, the steamers *Kathlamba* of North Shields, 6,382 tons, and the *Great City* of Bideford, 6,999 tons gross, a Ropner-built ship launched in 1914. Two days later, the Wilson Line steamer *Kelso*, 1,292 tons, was towed in with her decks almost awash, to be followed on 27 June by the three-masted schooner *A. B. Sherman*, escorted by the armed trawler *Nancy Lee*. This American sailing ship of 510 tons had been caught supplying a U-boat with oil at sea. She was towed to Devonport, stripped down and then laid up at Fowey, where a local shipyard later rebuilt her as a four-master.

With so many losses, there were endless incidents worth recalling, but since all cannot be recounted here four incidents have been chosen, concerning a cross-section of shipping—a famous sailing ship, a warship, a liner and a tramp. The sailing ship was the *Fiery Cross, a* barque from Larvik, Norway, built in September 1878 by Connell & Co of Glasgow. This 1,448-ton Cape Horner was carrying oil from the United States when she was stopped by a submarine and her crew ordered to abandon ship. Her master rowed a dinghy across to the German vessel and demanded a receipt from her commander for the *Fiery Cross*, whose sinking was delayed for half an hour while this was being prepared. It read, 'I hereby certify that I have sunk the *Fiery Cross*, Capt. John Geddie, on 3

July 1915 at 3.0 pm as she had contraband aboard, i.e. lubricating oil for France. Signed, Forstman, H. Lieut. Cdr'. The seal on the document bore the words, 'Imperial Marine, His Majesty's Submarine U—' followed by a blank, the identification number having been erased.

Among the American escort destroyers based on Queenstown, southern Ireland, in 1917 was the USS *Jacob Jones*, commanded by Lt-Cdr David Bagley USN, brother of the first naval officer killed in the Spanish-American war. A Conyngham class, four-funnelled vessel built by the New York Steamboat Co in 1915, the *Jacob Jones* was in company with six other destroyers returning from convoy duty off Brest when she was hit in the stern by a torpedo at 4.25 pm on 6 December. She settled down very quickly and as the quarterdeck went under water, depth-charges, already primed and fused for action, rolled overboard and sank. Those of her 108 crew who could get on deck promptly leapt overboard, and took the full stomach-tearing impact of the explosive charges as they detonated, killing them outright and blowing a whaleboat and its occupants to smithereens. She sank in less than eight minutes, in a position roughly 25 miles SE of the Bishop, taking sixty-four men with her. The German submarine responsible, the *U-53*, then surfaced nearby, and obligingly radioed Land's End, asking them to send help for the survivors. Two of these were in such a bad way that Capt. Hans Rose had them taken aboard, and eventually landed them at Heligoland for medical attention. The same submarine was responsible for the sinking of the ex-German vessel *Housatonic*, south of the Bishop on 3 February that same year, but only after the survivors were well clear of their ship. The day before the *Housatonic* was sent to the bottom, Capt. Hans Rose had stopped a French sailing ship and ordered her crew to abandon the vessel, but on being told the lifeboats were so rotten that the men would never reach land in them, he allowed them to proceed unharmed.

The White Star liner *Persic*, of Liverpool, was torpedoed on 8 September 1918, almost a year after a sister-ship, the *Delphic*, a twin-screw vessel of 8,273 tons built by Harland & Wolff in 1897, had been sunk 135 miles south-west of Scilly, on 10 August 1917. The *Persic* was more fortunate, and survived her attack. She carried a crew of fifty-six and 2,108 troops when hit by a torpedo, but was abandoned without the loss of a single life, a remarkable feat which owed much to her master, Capt. Harvey's insistence on regular lifeboat drill ever since they had left New York in convoy. The first torpedo fired at her missed, but a second struck the port side and tore a hole 72 × 22 ft, completely flooding Nos 3 and 4 holds. The troops were later transferred from the ship's boats and rafts to destroyer escorts and landed at Plymouth, the *Persic* herself being towed into Crow Sound and saved.

A Pomeranian dog was the saving of an entire crew on 1 July 1915, after the 4,656-ton steamer *Caucasian* had been attacked. Seventeen shells were fired into the vessel when she turned and fled after being challenged, until finally, with her bridge, wheelhouse and steering gear shot away, she hove-to and her crew began to abandon ship. The dog, named Betty and a pet of Capt. Robinson of South Shields, was accidentally dropped into the sea as the boats were being manned, and struck out for the surfaced submarine, to be quickly followed by its master. When the captain caught up with his pet and put it on his shoulders, he found the submarine had come close alongside and was told by her commander that he had intended to machine-gun the crew for not stopping when ordered, but had now changed his mind because of the captain's brave rescue of his dog. Before the war, the *Caucasian* had been stranded on the north coast of Cornwall, at Cape Cornwall, during fog on 30 May 1906, but had been towed off by the tug *Dragon* and the *Lady of the Isles*, which got the steamer in to Cardiff for repairs.

After the *Great City* was brought into St Mary's Roads in 1917, the stench of rotting grain was appalling. Four men died from the gas whilst clearing choked pumps on board, and after she had left for Liverpool on 25 September to have her torpedo damage repaired, it was learnt that she had had to put into Holyhead en route to land the corpses of another four men killed in the same way. Yet another three died in Liverpool docks from the same cause. In marked contrast was the steamer *Eastgate* of London, brought in by tugs after being torpedoed off the Bishop on 16 August 1917. Of 4,277 tons gross, the *Eastgate* was outward bound for the United States with a 'goodwill' cargo of luxury items, consisting of cosmetics, medical requisites, perfume, Paris fashions, fur coats and lingerie. Bundles of silk stockings, lace by the mile, hair dye, cough mixture, toothpaste and scent by the gallon washed out of her, and was much sought after by the women of the islands. Eau-de-Cologne in quart bottles, skin creams, Houbigant and Dior perfumes worth hundreds of pounds, it all washed about amongst the rocks between Samson and Tresco, scenting the islands in another and much more pleasant manner.

The last of the World War I casualties in the vicinity of Scilly were the *Rio Mondego*, the *Galway Castle*, the *Atlantico* and the *Montfort*. Damaged by a submarine's gunfire and abandoned on 1 September 1918, the *Rio Mondego*, a Portuguese sailing vessel, was later towed to St Mary's and beached on the eastern side of Stoney Island. She was carrying a cargo of port wine valued at £¼ million, some of which leaked out through the shell holes and into the sea, possibly an even more acceptable smell than that from either the *Great City* or the *Eastgate*! After being torpedoed on 13 September, the Union Castle steamer *Galway Castle* broke in half and sank, and the *Atlantico*, another Portuguese sailing ship, was shelled and sunk at 2.0 pm on 30 September. Two of her boats were towed in by the St Agnes lifeboat, with one dead seaman and a badly injured boy aboard. The *Montfort*, a Canadian Pacific Steamship Co vessel, was also sunk by a submarine some distance off Scilly to the west on 3 October, the last before the armistice was signed on 11 November.

Between the two world wars, offshore wrecks continued to occur, the majority of which have been mentioned in previous chapters. Those which have not include the wooden, three-masted schooner *Optimist*, lost off Scilly in March 1922. Built at Newfoundland in 1919 for A.E. Hickman of St Johns, she was of 130 tons gross and 100 ft overall in length. In 1927 another schooner, the 198 tons gross *Gougou* of Vannes, was in distress after being dismasted during a gale on 22 December. She drifted helpless for twenty hours, until sighted by the *Westphalia*, a German steamer, during the evening of the 23rd. Alerted by radio, the St Mary's lifeboat was launched and found the vessel only 300 yds SSE of the Seven Stones, waterlogged and in complete darkness. Her crew were taken off and landed back at the islands, after which the Trinity House steamer *Mermaid* set out from Penzance to find the derelict. When located ten miles further east, the *Gougou* already had a Dutch tug standing by her, the tug having attempted a tow but failed. Two men from the Trinity House vessel went aboard the schooner, passed a hawser across and both ships reached Penzance without further incident. During World War 2, when all merchant ships were armed and sailed in convoys, escorted by naval ships and aircraft when close to land, the 'deep-water' wrecks were well beyond the Isles of Scilly, and so outside the coverage of this book.

New Years Eve of 1961 saw the 7,660 tons gross *Indian Navigator* of Calcutta rocked by a violent explosion in No 4 hold when sixty miles south and west of the Scillies. A fire immediately followed and a distress call went out, to be answered by the Blue Funnel *Menesthems*, the Hamburg-Amerika liner *Dalerdyck* and the *Indian Success*, a sister-ship of the distressed vessel. Although the *Indian Navigator* was abandoned in appalling conditions of sea and wind, only one life was lost. Later, thirteen of the crew of the *Indian Success* went aboard the *Indian Navigator* to fight the fire. During the night of 2 January, there was a second violent explosion deep inside the ship and half a minute later she rolled over and sank, taking the entire salvage party to their deaths. Owned by the India Steamship Co of Calcutta, the *Indian Navigator* had been launched in 1944 by the Californian Shipbuilding Co of Los Angeles as the USSR

The wreck of the deelict barque *James Armstrong* lying just off the quay in Hugh Town harbour. Brought in pilots on 3 March 1875, she was found bottom up off Scilly. Her cargo of mahogany was worth £8,000, the salvors claiming three-quarters.

Victory, one of the 'standard' classes of vessel built during the second world war and commonly known as 'Victory' ships. Of all-welded construction, the *Indian Navigator* was a single-screw, steam-turbine vessel with an overall length of 455 ft.

Incidents concerning the sea and ships continue to the present day, and a lifeboat at Scilly is still as much a necessity as it has ever been. At 6.48 am on 22 May 1967, the *Guy and Clare Hunter* was launched to go to the aid of the motor-yacht *Braemar*. The wind was WSW force seven, gusting to force nine with a rough sea and bad visibility, when Coxswain Lethbridge set a course to intercept the *Braemar*, some twenty-eight miles from the Bishop. By the time the lifeboat arrived on the scene, the MV *Trader* had already attempted a tow but abandoned the attempt, and eventually asked the St Mary's boat to pass a second line for them, but this too was abandoned. The lifeboat then took the *Braemar* in tow and managed to shorten the distance to Newlyn before the leaking motor-yacht settled lower in the sea and took a dangerous list to starboard. Slipping the tow, the coxswain of the *Guy and*

Clare Hunter placed the lifeboat alongside the sinking vessel and in a brilliant display of seamanship took off fifteen men and one woman, leaving the yacht's master and two crew still aboard. The tow was then resumed in almost impossible conditions since the wind was now gusting force ten, but eventually both vessels reached Mounts Bay and the safety of Newlyn harbour. For this gallant service, one silver and two bronze medals were awarded to members of the lifeboat's crew.

Grim reminders of shipwreck still come ashore on the islands' beaches, one recent example being the sternboard of the *Venus*, a French trawler sunk on 8 September 1969. A more tragic reminder was the body of a man wearing only a life-jacket, washed up on Tresco on 25 February 1970. The number on the life-jacket, DI1714, and other evidence proved beyond doubt that the dead man came from the French trawler *Jean Gougy*. This 246 tons gross

Laden with zinc-ore, the Cypriot motor vessel *Poleire lies* sunk on Little Kettle Rock, north-west of Tresco island, 15 April 1970

vessel had put into Newlyn on 20 February to land the mate, who had a suspected fracture of the arm. She sailed again to fish over the weekend, returned for the mate three days later, but was never heard of again. Bunks, a ladder, timber and insulating material of the type used in a trawler's fish-hold, drifted down through Broad Sound that week, which suggested that the trawler had struck the Western Rocks and sunk with the loss of her fourteen crew. Another French trawler with an almost identical name, the *Jeanne Gougy*, also met a tragic end in Cornish waters. This was on 3 November 1962, when she struck Land's End and sank with the loss of twelve lives.

The most recent loss of any size, up to the time of writing, was that of the Cypriot motor-vessel *Poleire* of 1,599 tons gross, which struck the Little Kettle rock, north-west of Tresco on

15 April 1970 in dense fog. Carrying a cargo of zinc ore, she was bound for Gdynia, Poland, from Ireland when she went ashore less than a mile from the Round Island lighthouse, having failed to hear its fog signal. Within a week the vessel broke in two and settled on the sea bed.

An old island prayer, attributed to the Rev Troutbeck of St Mary's says, 'We pray thee, O Lord, not that wrecks should happen, but that if they should happen, that thou wilt guide them into the Scillies for the benefit of the poore inhabitants'.

That his prayer has been answered in full measure this book bears witness. Happily in recent years, entries in this grim record have become few and far between, and though it can never be closed so long as the elements endure and man continues to be his own worst enemy, the time may one day come when it will be remembered only as a part of the islands' history, and a mere fraction of the toll the sea has always taken in the coastal waters of the British Isles.

Source Notes

Chapter One

1 *Ancient Monuments of the Isles of Scilly*, p 3
2 Ibid
3 *Victoria History of Cornwall*
   (Maritime Appendix)
4 *A Natural and Historical Account of Scilly*,
   p 9
5 Ibid, p 63
6 Ibid, p 64
7 *Victoria History of Cornwall*
   (Maritime Appendix)
8 *A Natural and Historical Account of Scilly*,
   p 65
9 *A Natural and Historical Account of Scilly*,
   p 65
10 Ibid
11 Ibid
12 *Victoria History of Cornwall*
   (Maritime Appendix)
13 *Lighthouses, their History and Romance*,
   (1895)
14 Ibid
15 Ibid
16 *Tour Through Great Britain*, Defoe D. 1724
   Hen. VIII IV, pt 2
17 *Victoria History of Cornwall*
18 *Scillonian Magazine*, no 26, (June 1931)
19 *Cornish Magazine*, I. 1/2 Stowe MSS 865,
   f38
20 *Scillonian Magazine*, no 26, (June 1931)
21 *The Beautiful Islets of Britaine*, (1860)
22 Report to *HRH the Prince of Wales concerning
   a refuge at the I.O.S.*, (1810), p 10
23 Ibid
24 *The Beautiful Islets of Britaine*, (1860)

Chapter Two

1 *Western Luminary*, (17 April 1821)
2 *Scilly and the Scillonians*, (1907)
3 Ms. Rawlinson. A195a—Bodleian Library
4 *Sherborne Mercury*, (May 1875)

5 Extract from a paper by James H. Cooke,
   FSA, read to Society of Antiquities,
   London, 1 February 1883

Chapter Three

1 *I went to Tristan*, (1941)
2 *Falmouth Packet* newspaper, (16 August
   1909)

Chapter Four

1 Chope, P. *Early Tours in Devon and
   Cornwall* (Leyland). (Reprint 1967)
2 *A survey of the ancient and present state of the
   Isles of Scilly*, Troutbeck
3 *Falmouth and Penryn Weekly Times*, (24
   January 1874)
4 *A survey of the ancient and present state of the
   Isles of Scilly*, Troutbeck
5 Chope, P. *Early Tours in Devon and
   Cornwall* (Leyland). (Reprint 1967)
6 *Account of the Isles of Scilly*
7 *A view of the present state of the Scilly Islands*
8 Whitfield, H. *Scilly and its Legends*
9 Deposition Book 1885/1900, St Mary's
   Custom House

Chapter Five

1 *Portrait of the Isles of Scilly*, (1967)
2 *Morning Herald*, (19 December 1798)
3 Greville and Hamilton MSS. Brit. Mus.
   42069-82 (Additional)
4 *Royal National Lifeboat Institution Annual
   Report*, (1871)
5 Chope, P. *Early Tours in Devon and
   Cornwall* (Leyland) (Reprint 1967)

Chapter Seven

1 Gill, C. Brooker, F. and Soper, T. *The Wreck
   of the 'Torrey Canyon'*, Newton Abbot, 1967
2 Cowan, E. *Oil and Water*, (1969)

Appendix:
Wreck statistics

Since man first ventured on the sea, the greatest hazard has been that of sinking, a danger as real today as it was five thousand years ago. Despite steel hulls, watertight bulkheads, radar and other modern innovations which have combined greatly to reduce the annual total of casualties, ships continue to be lost by collision, stranding and wreck with almost frightening regularity. Throughout this book and its two companion volumes which have encompassed the more tragic or dramatic shipwrecks in Cornwall, it has been emphasised that these are but a proportion of the total. It would require many such volumes to record details of the known wrecks around the south-western peninsula of Britain, since they number in excess of 15,000, and countless others will forever remain anonymous. Yet, by comparison to the numbers lost on Britain's east coast, they are but a fraction, so that the overall number of vessels wrecked around the British Isles must now exceed an appalling total of at least 100,000.

Although one might imagine differently, it is an indisputable fact that no country in the world has a central or complete record of ships lost on its coastline, simply because there has never been a requirement. Only in recent years has there been an upsurge of interest in wreck information, and have people begun to regret that their forefathers did not trouble to record shipping losses in detail. Great Britain is more fortunate than most countries in that records are available for the past three hundred years at least. Lloyd's of London, for example, have shipping information dating back to the mid 1740s, and records of the Royal National Lifeboat Institution and the Board of Trade date from the mid-1800s; but, to compile even a modest record of wrecks in one particular area would require many years of patient research and recording, gleaning and assembling what one can from the above records, plus that to be found in newspapers, journals, war casualty lists, public records, court-rolls, and other often obscure sources. Apart from commercial salvage and navigation, the value of this information might appear to be purely academic, but is a subject now playing an ever increasing role in planning decisions, determining the location of offshore sewer outfalls, undersea telephone cables, gas pipe lines and offshore exploration. To this end the Royal Commission on the Historic Monuments of England in 1992 launched a new initiative, which was the inauguration of their Maritime Archaeological Record (MAR), to compliment an existing National Archaeological Record (NAR). The M.A.R. will be a record of all maritime related sites, not only submerged dwellings and fortifications, but old waterfronts, quays, jetties, harbours, fish-traps, locks etc. and of course shipwrecks, to which the author and his wife are making a substancial contribution.

The first Board of Trade report submitted to parliament in 1851, giving official shipping casualty figures for the entire country, stated that 692 vessels were wrecked during the preceding twelve months. By 1852, the annual total had risen to 1,115 ships lost along with 900 lives, but this particular year was exceptional. In January alone, a disastrous gale which lasted five days, caused the loss of 257 vessels together with 486 of their passengers and crews. Two years later, 1,549 persons died in 893 wrecks and ninety-four serious collisions, and 1856 saw 1,153 losses with 521 deaths as a direct result. Broken down into categories of ships, these show the marked predominance of sail:

Table I Types of vessels lost on the U.K. coast in 1856 including what is now the Irish Republic.

(a)	Sailing ships lost in deep water	546
(b)	Sailing ships lost in coastal waters	432
(c)	Sailing colliers lost	141
(d)	Steamships lost	34

The next table covering the period 1854-56, which compares losses in different coastal areas, clearly shows the point made earlier, that the east coast has claimed a far greater percentage of wreck than elsewhere in the British Isles:

Table 2 Total number of wrecks in various coastal regions for 1854 and 1856

	Geographic boundaries	1854	1856
(a)	Between Greenock and Land's End	164	307
(b)	Between Land's End and Dungeness	38	119
(c)	Between Dungeness and the Pentland Firth	350	506
(d)	On the coast of Northern Ireland	66	155
(e)	On the Isles of Scilly	5	12
(f)	On the island of Lundy	2	11

Frightful though these losses were, it must be remembered that these figures indicate only the ships lost around the United Kingdom coastline. British-registered ships and seamen lost elsewhere in the world and therefore not taken into account in these tables, amounted in 1856 for example, to 1,143 vessels, increasing to 1,170 in 1858.

During October 1859, the coast of Great Britain was hit by a tempest which became known as the 'Royal Charter' gale, the worst on record to have struck its shores. It took its name from the tragic loss of the Liverpool & Australian Steam Navigation Co's passenger vessel, *Royal Charter,* in Moelfre Bay, North Wales, in which 459 persons were lost out of a total complement of 498. The gale was at its height on the 24th, and during that twenty-four hour period 195 vessels were wrecked around the country. Neither the wind nor sea returned to anything like normal until 1 November, when the country was shocked to learn that during the ten-day period the sea had claimed 248 ships and 686 lives.

An analysis of the number of lives lost as a result of wrecks during the next ten-year period is as follows:

Table 3 Loss of life in wrecks around the British Isles between 1860-69

	Geographic boundaries	1860	1867	Total 1860-69
(a)	Fern Islands-Flamborough Head	25	30	418
(b)	Flamborough Head-North Foreland	107	152	887
(c)	North Foreland-St Catherine's	31	35	250
(d)	St Catherine's-Start Point	12	14	250
(e)	Start Point-Land's End	12	108	319
(f)	Land's End-Hartland plus Scilly	10	58	394
(g)	Hartland-St David's Head	82	61	576
(h)	St David's Head-Lambay Island	3	54	416
(i)	Lambay Island-Mull of Cantire	50	165	914
(j)	Cape Wrath-Buchan-ness	44	14	262
(k)	Buchan-ness-Fern Islands	21	9	233
(l)	All other parts of coast together	62	135	838

These staggering figures continued to escalate, with only minor fluctuations, until they reached a peak for sailing vessels in the 1860s and steam in the 1880s. Unfortunately, the figures compiled by the Board of Trade for presentation to the House of Commons were not consistent in their layout or presentation, so that it is often difficult to differentiate between

British and foreign losses, and whether or not these were at home or abroad. They are made even more complicated by volumes of statistics as to whether they were classed as founderings, strandings, collisions, total wrecks, or losses as the result of fire or other causes. It is possible, however, to state that the peak years for sail and steam losses appear to have been 1864 and 1880 respectively. The total number of ships of all types, both British and foreign, lost on the coast of the United Kingdom in 1864 was 1,741, with 516 lives. For 1880, the figures were 1,303 and 2,100. By comparison, the trend towards steamers carrying larger crews and more passengers is shown by the fact that by 1909, the annual losses were down to 733 ships, but the deaths had increased to 4,738.

Throughout the history of shipwreck, a few specific vessels have attracted great attention, usually due to the heavy loss of life involved. Indisputably, the greatest maritime loss on the British coast was that of Sir Clowdisley Shovell's ships in 1707, but though most people in Britain will know of the *Royal George*, sunk at Spithead in 1782 with over 600 drowned, and of the liner *Titanic*, which took 1,498 lives when she foundered in the North Atlantic in 1912, literally thousands of earlier but comparable disasters are now unremembered. In November 1703, an entire fleet of British warships under Rear-Admiral Beaumont, thirteen in all, was wrecked on or near the Goodwin's and 1,200 officers and men perished. HMS *Ardent* blew up off Corsica in 1794 killing her entire crew of 500; the warship *Couragoux* was lost off the Barbary coast two years later with 440 men, and the *Queen Charlotte*, with 673 dead, off Leghorn in 1800.

In British waters, the *York* went down in the North Sea during 1813 with 491 lost, the *Royal Adelaide* off Margate with 428 persons in 1850; a steamer, the *City of Glasgow*, went missing with 480 on board and was never heard of again; the *Northfleet* off Dungeness in 1873 with 293 victims, and others. But pride of place in this macabre record must surely go to the *Wilhelm Gustloff*, a German steamer of 25,484 tons, which was torpedoed and sunk by a Russian submarine in the Baltic on 18 February 1945. Carrying German navy technicians and evacuees, she took to the bottom with her no less than 4,120 people.

Bibliography

Alderidge, W. *Hobnails and Seaboots*, (1956)

Baring-Gould, S. *Book of the West*, vol 2, (1899)

Baring-Gould, S. *Cornish Characters and Strange Events*, (1908)

Borlase, W. *Observations on the ancient and present state of the Isles of Scilly*, Oxford, (1756)

Boulay, J du. 'Wrecks of the Isles of Scilly', *Mariner's Mirror reprint*, vol 45, no 4 (1959) and vol 46 (1960)

Carew, R. *The survey of Cornwall* (1602, reprinted 1811)

Carvel, J.L. *Stephen of Linthouse. 1750-1950*, (1950)

Coate, M. *Cornwall in the great Civil War and interregnum. 1642–1660*, Oxford, (1933)

Colledge. J.J. *Ships of the Royal Navy*, vol 1, Newton Abbot, (1969)

Cooke, J.H. *The shipwreck of Sir Cloudesley Shovell*, (1883)

Course, Capt A. *Painted Ports*, (1961)

Courtney, L.C. *Guide to Penzance and its neighbourhood including the Islands of Scilly*, (1845)

Cowan, E. *Oil and Water*, (1969)

Dawson, A.J. *Britain's lifeboats*, (1923)

Dendry, W.C. *The beautiful islets of Britaine*, (1857)

Domville-Fife, C. *Epics of the square-rigged ships*, (1958)

Dorrien-Smith, C. *Shipwrecks of the Isles of Scilly*, (1949)

Dunbar, J. *The Lost Land*, (1958)

Elliot-Burns, L.E. *Medieval Cornwall*,(1955)

Esquires, A. *Cornwall and its Coasts*, (1865)

Fagan, H.S. 'The Scilly Isles', *Fraser's Magazine* reprint

Gibson, A. & H. *The Isles of Scilly*, (1925)

Gill, C. Booker, F. Soper, T. *The Wreck Of The 'Torrey Canyon'*, Newton Abbot, (1967)

Gillis, R. *A Sea Miscellany of Cornwall*, Bristol, (1969)

Grant, R. M. *U-Boats Destroyed*, (1964)

Green, E. *Isles of Ictis*, (1906)

Greenhill, B. *The Merchant Schooners*, vols 1 & 2, Newton Abbott, (1968)

Grigson, G. *The Scilly Isles*, (1948)

Halliwell, J.C. *Rambles in western Cornwall*, (1861)

Hamilton-Jenkin, A. *Cornwall and its People*, (1945)

Hardy, J. *Lighthouses, their History and Romance*, (1895)'I

Harper, C.G. *The Cornish coast and Isles of Scilly*, (1910)

Heath, R. *A Natural and Historical account of the islands of Scilly*, (1750, reprinted 1967)

Henderson, C. *Essays in Cornish History*

Hitchens, F. & Drew, S. *A History of Cornwall*, (1816)

Hocking, C. *A Dictionary of Disasters at Sea in the Age of Steam,1824-1962*, vols 1 & 2, (1969)

Jameson, W. *The Most Formidable Thing*, (1965)

Jellicoe, G.A. *A Landscape Charter of the Isles of Scilly*

Jenkin, A.K.H. *Cornish Seafarers*

Kay, E. *Isles of Flowers*, (1956)

Larn, R. & Carter, C. *Cornish Shipwrecks, the South Coast*, Newton Abbot, (1969)

Le Flemming, H. M. *Warships of World War I*, (1965)

Lewis, H.A. *St Martins, St Helens and Tean*, (1900)

Lubbock, B. *The Last of the Windjammers*, vols 1 & 2, (1963)

Magalotti, L. *Travels of Cosmo, the 3rd Grand Duke of Tuscany, through England and Wales in the reign of Charles II*, (English translation 1821)

Mais, S. P. B. *Isles of the Islands*, (1934)

Maybee, R. *Sixty-eight Years Experience of the Scilly Islands*, (1883)

Mitchell, W. & Sawyer, L. 'British Standard Ships of World War I',I *Sea Breezes*, (1968)3

Mitchell, W. & Sawyer, L. 'Empire Ships of World War II, *Sea Breezes*, (1965)

Morris, R. *Island Treasure*, (1969)

Mothersole, J. *The Isles of Scilly*, (1910)

Mumford, C. *Portrait of the Isles of Scilly*, (1967)

Noall, C. *Cornish Lights and Shipwrecks*, Truro, (1968)

Noall, C. & Farr, G. *Wreck and Rescue round the Cornish Coast*,

vol 2, The story of the Land's End lifeboats, Truro, (1965)

North, I.W. *A week at the Isles of Scilly*, (1850)

O'Neil, B.H. *Ancient Monuments of the Isles of Scilly*, (1961)

Owen, J.G. *Faire Lyonesse*, Bideford, (1897)

Page, W. Ed. *The Victoria History of the counties of England (Cornwall)*, (1906)

Parkes, O. *Ships of the Royal Navy*, (1932)

Pearse, R. *The Ports and Harbours of Cornwall*, (1964)

Pearson, Chope. *Early Tours in Devon and Cornwall*, Newton Abbot, (1967)

Polwhele, R. *History of Cornwall*, (1804)

Quixley, R.C. *Antique Maps of Cornwall and the Isles of Scilly*, (Reprint, 1966)

Rennell, J. *Observations on the current to the west of Scilly*, (1873)

Roskill, Capt S.W. *The War at Sea*, vols 1–4, (1954)

Smith, G.C. *The Extreme Misery of the Off-islands*, (1818)

Smith, G.C. *The Scilly Isles and the Famine*, (1828)

Smith, G.C. *The Cassiterides*, (1863)

Strike, F. *Cornish Shipwrecks*, Porthleven, (1965)

Thurstan, P.C. *Cassiterides and Ictis, where are they?* (1909)

Tucker, B. *Report to HRH The Prince of Wales, concerning the formation of a safe roadstead at the Isles of Scilly*, (1810)

Tonkin, J.C. *The Homeland Guide for the Isles of Scilly*, (1900)

Tonkin, J. & R. *Guide to the Isles of Scilly*, Penzance, (1887)

Tonkin, J. & Prescott. *Lyonesse, a Hand book for the Isles of Scilly*

Trengrouse, H. *Shipwreck Investigated*, Penaluna, (1818)

Troutbeck, J. *A Survey of the Ancient and Present State of the Isles of Scilly*, Sherborne, (1796)

Uren, J.G. 'Scilly and the Scillonians', *Western Morning News*, Plymouth, (1907)

Ward, C.S. *South Devon and a Description of the Isles of Scilly*, (1702)

White, W. *A Londoner's Walk to the Land's End, and a Tour of the Scillies*, (1855)

Whitfield, H.J. *Scilly and its Legends*, (1852)

Wood, C.W. 'At the Scilly Isles', *Argosy Magazine*, vol 17/18 (1800) (1850)

Woodley, G. *A View of the Present State of the Isles of Scilly*, (1822)

Woodley, G. *Narrative of the Loss of the steamer 'Thames' on the rocks of Scilly*

NEWSPAPERS, JOURNALS, ETC

Alfred West of England Journal & General Advertiser, 1816-31

Commercial Shipping & General Advertiser for West Cornwall, from 1867

Cornish Magazine, Falmouth, various issues, 1960-68

Cornishman, from 1878

Cornish Telegraph, from 1851, and *Tidings*

Cornish Times and General Advertiser, from 1857

Daily Western Mercury, from 1860

Devonport Independent and Plymouth and Stonehouse Gazette, from 1833

Falmouth Packet, from 1832

Falmouth and Penryn Weekly Times Felix Farley's Bristol Journal, from 1714

Lifeboat, Journal of the Royal National Lifeboat Institution

Lloyd's Universal Register, various, 1764-1967

Mercantile Navy List and Maritime Directory, 1939

Royal Cornwall Gazette, 1803-1952

Sherborne Mercury St Austell Gazette, 1870-78

Sea Breezes, various, 1932-67

Trewman's Exeter Flying Post, from 1763

West Briton, from 1810

Western Independent Western Luminary & Family Newspaper, from 1827

Western Morning News, from 1860

Index of shipwrecks

This index includes only those ships which were lost by shipwreck in or around the Isles of Scilly, and does not include those which went ashore and were refloated, or were brought in as derelicts from offshore. Page references in italic denote illustrations. Ships with no page reference are unmentioned in the text.

Abbreviations used to denote ship types are as follows:

BR	brig	FR	full-rigged ship	PC	pilot cutter
BN	brigantine	GA	galliot	PD	paddle-steamer
BQ	barque	KT	ketch	PE	privateer
BE	barquentine	LC	landing-craft	SL	sloop
CA	cargo/passenger, paddle	LU	lugger	SM	smack
CM	chasse-maree	HM	man o'war, unspecified	SN	snow
CU	cutter	H2	man o'war 2nd. rate	SS	steamship
DA	dandy	H3	man o'war 3rd. rate	TP	transport, sail
EI	east indiaman	H4	man o'war 4th. rate	TG	tug
EP	east indiaman, packet	H5	man o'war 5th. rate	WI	west indiaman
FL	fishing vessel, MFV	H7	fireship	WS	warship, general
FM	fishing trawler, SS	MV	motor-vessel	ZZ	any other type, see text for
FS	fishing vessel, sail	PK	packet vessel		details

No.	Ship Name	Ship type	Date lost	Location	Page No
201	Monmouth	SV	27/02/1795	Not known	
581	Mouette	SC	20/08/1896	Offshore	
660	Mysotis	SC	09/09/1916	Offshore	
671	Naiad	FR	15/12/1916	Offshore	
250	Nancy	BR	04/01/1809	St Helen's island	
164	Nancy	SV	05/09/1783	Annet island	
64	Nancy	SV	00/00/1743	Samson island	
219	Nancy	SV	08/02/1799	Not known	
161	Nancy	EP	04/03/1783	Western Rocks	31
61	Nancy	SV	09/03/1742	Tresco island	91
697	Nascent	SS	25/08/1917	Offshore	
541	Nellie	BN	26/03/1886	Western Rocks	51; 132
486	Nelson	BQ	07/10/1870	Seven Stones	121
76	Neptune	SV	25/04/1755	Not known	
370	Nerina	BR	18/11/1840	St Mary's island	65
269	New Friends	SV	02/09/1812	Offshore	
324	New Jane	SL	08/01/1828	Western Rocks	
152	New York	BR	00/00/1782	St Mary's island	69
718	Ngaroma	SS	08/08/1942	Seven Stones	
379	Nickerie	BQ	21/11/1843	Western Rocks	32
124	Nimrod	SV	17/01/1775	Offshore	
574	Niord	SS	13/03/1892	Offshore	
721	Noel	FL	20/09/1946	Offshore	
466	Noel Raphael	BR	23/03/1867	Seven Stones	
678	Noorderdijk	SS	22/02/1917	Offshore	136
682	Normanna	SS	22/02/1917	Offshore	
92	Nostra Senora de Muriel	SV	00/10/1760	Not known	
647	Nugget	SS	31/07/1915	Offshore	66
588	Nyanza	LU	26/05/1898	Western Rocks	
255	Nymph	BR	23/11/1809	Samson island	
327	Ocean	SN	04/01/1829	Western Rocks	
583	Ocean Belle	SC	29/11/1896	Offshore	132
453	Ocean Queen	BQ	17/05/1865	Offshore	91
158	Oldenbruger	BR	24/01/1783	Tresco island	
299	Olive	SV	12/02/1819	Seven Stones	
357	Osiris	BQ	29/05/1838	Western Rocks	34–5
430	Osvetitel	BQ	14/07/1860	Maiden Bower	82
480	Otto	BN	06/12/1869	St Mary's Roads	78
479	Oxus	FR	31/08/1869	Seven Stones	121
358	Pacquebot de Cayenne	BQ	27/11/1838	Crow Sound	108
234	Padstow	SV	24/12/1804	Not known	
391	Palinurus	BQ	27/12/1848	White island	103
654	Palmgrove	SS	22/08/1915	Offshore	135
585	Palmos	SC	07/04/1897	Offshore	
594	Parame	BQ	26/10/1899	Scilly Rock	
464	Patrie	BR	17/03/1867	Offshore	132
428	Pauline	SC	18/02/1860	Crow Sound	111
643	Pelham	SS	13/06/1915	Offshore	
257	Perseus	SV	27/01/1810	Samson island	
236	Perseverance	BR	14/11/1805	Seven Stones	119
279	Perseverance	SV	17/01/1815	Not known	
138	Pheasant	BR	16/01/1780	Not known	
169	Phoenix	SC	06/01/1785	Not known	
25	Phoenix	EI	11/01/1680	Western Rocks	32
33	Phoenix	H7	22/10/1707	Tresco island	
599	Phosphor	SS	13/07/1904	Offshore	133
612	Phyllis Anne	FE	29/04/1909	Offshore	
623	Pierre L'Abbe	SC	25/05/1912	Bryher island	
704	Pincher	DY	24/07/1918	Seven Stones	127
571	Plato	SS	29/02/1892	Offshore	132
371	Plenty	SC	03/12/1840	Eastern isles	
540	Plump	CU	30/12/1885	Samson island	
613	Plympton	SS	14/08/1909	St Agnes island	*51*; 51–2

General Index